THINKING
FOR
POWERFUL
LIVING

BOB PHILLIPS

HARVEST HOUSE PUBLISHERS
Eugene, Oregon 97402

POWERFUL THINKING FOR POWERFUL LIVING

Copyright © 1991 by Harvest House Publishers
Eugene, Oregon 97402

Library of Congress Cataloging-in-Publication Data

Phillips, Bob, 1940–
    Powerful thinking for powerful living / Bob Phillips.
    ISBN 0-89081-894-0
    1. Quotations, English.   I. Title
PN6081.P48   1991
082—dc20   91-11354
                                                   CIP

Printed in the United States of America.

Dedicated to

Charles E. Jones

*A man who loves books
and great quotes...
A man who has influenced
me in practical living...*

A tremendous friend!

Introduction

Putting together *Powerful Thinking for Powerful Living* was a labor of love and joy. Many times during the writing, I would catch myself smiling at the down-to-earth insights into human nature.

This book contains over 2,400 quotations on over 850 different topics. I attempted to identify the author of each quotation. These individuals may not have been the original person to initiate the quote but they have been attributed with it. You will note that I have included famous persons and people that few know.

Every now and then you will note a quotation from an infamous person. These were included not because I agree with them, but to cause the reader to realize the power and influence that negative people have had in this world.

I hope that you will have much enjoyment as you read these great thoughts. I also hope that the practical advice will stimulate and challenge you. I would encourage you to share these wise words and witty sayings with your family and friends. We only keep that which we give away.

> If you find a wise sentence or apt phrase, commit it to your memory.
>
> ~ *Henry Sidney*

> I quote others only in order the better to express myself.   ~*Michel de Montaigne*

Have a good time,

Bob Phillips
Fresno, California

——— ABILITY ———

Behind an able man there are always other able men.
~ *Chinese Proverb*

You can always tell luck from ability by its duration.

There is something that is much scarcer, something finer by far, something rarer than ability. It is the ability to recognize ability.   ~ *Elbert Hubbard*

As we advance in life, we learn the limits of our abilities.
~ *J.A. Froude*

We judge ourselves by what we feel capable of doing, while others judge us by what we have already done.
~ *Henry Wadsworth Longfellow*

The winds and waves are always on the side of the ablest navigators.
~ *Edward Gibbon*

Ability is of little account without opportunity.
~ *Napoleon*

——— ABSENCE ———

If your absence won't make any difference, your presence won't either.   ~*Decision*

Absence makes the heart grow fonder.

~*Thomas Haynes Bayly*

——— ABSURDITY ———

Every absurdity has a champion to defend it.

~*Oliver Goldsmith*

——— ACCEPTANCE ———

He who doesn't accept the conditions of life sells his soul.   ~*Charles Baudelaire*

When we have accepted the worst, we have nothing more to lose. And that automatically means we have everything to gain.   ~*Dale Carnegie*

——— ACCOMPLISHMENT ———

No matter what your lot in life, build something on it.

Lord, grant that I may always desire more than I can accomplish.   ~*Michelangelo*

—— **ACHIEVEMENT** ——

If you want a place in the sun, you will have to expect some blisters.

He who wants to get to the top must get off his bottom.

—— **ACQUAINTANCE** ——

Acquaintance: A person whom we know well enough to borrow from, but not well enough to lend to.

~ Ambrose Bierce

—— **ACTION** ——

To put your ideas into action is the most difficult thing in the world. *~ Goethe*

Action may not always bring happiness; but there is no happiness without action.

~ Benjamin Disraeli

—— **ACTIONS** ——

People may doubt what you say, but they will always believe what you do.

Don't forget that people will judge you by your actions, not your intentions. You may have a heart of gold—but so does a hard-boiled egg.

Actions speak louder than words—and are just as apt to be misquoted or misinterpreted.

——— ACTORS ———

You can pick out actors by the glazed look that comes to their eyes when the conversation wanders away from themselves.

——— ADAM AND EVE ———

Adam and Eve had many advantages, but the principal one was that they escaped teething.

~ Mark Twain

——— ADULTERY ———

But the man who commits adultery is an utter fool, for he destroys his own soul.

~ Proverbs 6:32

In every affair consider what precedes and what follows. *~ Epictetus*

Can a man hold fire against his chest and not be burned? *~ Proverbs 6:27*

ADVERSARY

Next to a happy family and a few good friends, the best human gift that God can give to any man is a worthy adversary.

ADVERSITY

You are a poor specimen if you can't stand the pressure of adversity.　　　*~ Proverbs 24:10*

Adversity causes some men to break, others to break records.　　　*~ William A. Ward*

* Adversity is the only diet that will reduce a fat head.

There is no education like adversity.

~ Benjamin Disraeli

Prosperity is a great teacher; adversity is a greater. Possession pampers the mind; privation trains and strengthens it.　　　*~ William Hazlitt*

Adversity makes men think of God.

~ Livy

In time of prosperity friends will be plenty;
In times of adversity not one in twenty.

~ English Proverb

———— ADVERTISING ————

When business is good, it pays to advertise; when business is bad, you've got to advertise.

Of the ninety percent of businesses that fail, they fail in the area of advertising.

Doing business without advertising is like winking at a girl in the dark: You know what you are doing but nobody else does.   *~ Ed Howe*

———— ADVICE ————

How is it possible to expect mankind to take advice when they will not so much as take warning?

~ Jonathan Swift

Get all the advice you can and be wise the rest of your life.   *~ Proverbs 19:20*

Listen to this wise advice; follow it closely, for it will do you good, and you can pass it on to others: Trust in the Lord.   *~ Proverbs 22:17-19*

Timely advice is as lovely as gold apples in a silver basket.   *~ Proverbs 25:11*

You save a lot of unnecessary conversation if you remember that people are not going to take your advice unless you charge them for it.

Asking for advice is how some people trap you into expressing an opinion they can disagree with.

~Franklin P. Jones

It takes a great man to give sound advice tactfully, but a greater to accept it graciously.

~J.C. Macaulay

The trouble with giving advice is people want to repay you. *~Franklin P. Jones*

We give advice by the bucket, but take it by the grain. *~W.R. Alger*

The most unrewarding task in the world is trying to tell people the truth about themselves before they are ready to hear it; and even Aesop, who cast such truth in fable form, was eventually thrown off a cliff because his morals struck too close to home.

~Sydney Harris

Admonish your friends privately, but praise them openly. *~Publilius Syrus*

When a man comes to me for advice, I find out the kind of advice he wants—and I give it to him.

~Josh Billings

When a man seeks your advice he generally wants your praise. *~Lord Chesterfield*

A good scare is worth more to a man than good advice. ~ *Ed Howe*

—— **AFFECTIONS** ——

Above all else, guard your affections. For they influence everything else in your life.

~ *Proverbs 4:23*

—— **AGE** ——

It takes about ten years to get used to how old you are.

I am not young enough to know everything.

~ *Oscar Wilde*

Middle age is the time when a man is always thinking that in a week or two he will feel as good as ever.

~ *Don Marquis*

The ten best years of a woman's life are between the ages of twenty-nine and thirty.

~ *Peter Weiss*

Whenever a man's friends begin to compliment him about looking young, he may be sure that they think he is growing old. ~ *Washington Irving*

A man fools himself. He prays for a long life, and he fears old age. *~Chinese Proverb*

AGREEABLE

My idea of an agreeable person is a person who agrees with me. *~Benjamin Disraeli*

If you find a man who always agrees with you, you have to watch him, because he is apt to lie about other things too. *~Robert A. Cook*

If you wish to appear agreeable in society, you must consent to be taught many things which you know already. *~Charles Talleyrand*

AILMENTS

We are so fond of one another because our ailments are the same. *~Jonathan Swift*

AIRLINES

You can't fool all the people all the time, but the airplane schedules come pretty close.

ALARM CLOCK

An alarm clock is a device for awakening people who don't have small children.

—— ALCOHOL ——

Alcohol is used by a majority of the adult population and creates more problems than all other drugs combined. *~ Robert Elliott*

—— ALGEBRA ——

Stand firm in your refusal to remain conscious during algebra. In real life, I assure you, there is no such thing as algebra. *~ Fran Lebowitz*

—— ALONE ——

The human race is not alone in the universe . . . I am not alone. *~ Richard E. Byrd*

—— AMBITION ——

Ambition and death are alike in this: neither is ever satisfied. *~ Proverbs 27:20*

Keep away from people who try to belittle your ambitions. Small people always do that, but the really great make you feel that you too can become great.

~ Mark Twain

By working faithfully eight hours a day you may eventually get to be a boss and work twelve hours a day.

~ Robert Frost

There was a kid on the block who always wanted to be a pirate when he grew up. Today he is a doctor. He's lucky. Not every man realizes the ambitions of his youth.

——— AMERICA ———

The things that will destroy America are prosperity-at-any-price, safety-first instead of duty-first, the love of soft living, and the get-rich-quick theory of life.

~ *Theodore Roosevelt*

——— ANGELS ———

Man was created a little lower than the angels, and has been getting a little lower ever since.

~ *Josh Billings*

——— ANGER ———

Anger is just one letter short of danger.

Anger is quieted by a gentle word, just as fire is quenched by water.   ~ *Megiddo Message*

Keep away from angry, short-tempered men, lest you learn to be like them and endanger your soul.

~ *Proverbs 22:24, 25*

As the churning of cream yields butter, and a blow to the nose causes bleeding, so anger causes quarrels.

~*Proverbs 30:33*

In thy rage make no Persian decree which cannot be reversed or repealed; but rather Polonian laws, which (they say) last but three days.

~*Thomas Fuller*

When angry, count ten before you speak: if very angry, a hundred. ~*Thomas Jefferson*

Anger is a wind which blows out the lamp of the mind.

Anger: An acid that can do more harm to the vessel in which it is stored than to anything on which it is poured.

A chip on the shoulder usually comes from the block above it. ~*E. Roger Jones*

The greatest cure of anger is delay.

~*Seneca*

No man can think clearly when his fists are clenched.

~*George Jean Nathan*

Beware the fury of a patient man.

~*John Dryden*

Never forget what a man has said to you when he was angry. ~*Henry Ward Beecher*

I was angry with my friend:
I told my wrath, my wrath did end.
I was angry with my foe:
I told it not, my wrath did grow.

~ *William Blake*

——— **ANSWER** ———

A gentle answer turns away wrath, but harsh words cause quarrels.   ~ *Proverbs 15:1*

No answer is also an answer.

~ *German Proverb*

——— **ANT** ———

None preaches better than the ant, and she says nothing.   ~ *Benjamin Franklin*

——— **ANXIETY** ———

Up to a certain point anxiety is good, for it promotes action. Beyond that point we freeze any fixed attitudes or rush about without thinking deeply from one decision to another.   ~ *Jules Henry*

——— **APATHY** ———

All that is necessary for the forces of evil to win in the world is for enough good men to do nothing.

~ *Edmund Burke*

——— APPEARANCES ———

Appearances deceive and this one maxim is a standing rule: men are not what they seem.

~ Havard

——— APPEASE ———

An appeaser is one who feeds a crocodile hoping it will eat him last.   *~ Winston Churchill*

——— APPRECIATION ———

The deepest principle in human nature is the craving to be appreciated.   *~ William James*

You can't appreciate home till you've left it, money till it's spent, your wife till she's joined a woman's club, and Old Glory till you see it hanging on a broom stick of a consul in a foreign town.

~ O. Henry

——— APPROVAL ———

In my wide association in life, meeting with many and great men in various parts of the world, I have yet to find the man, however great or exalted his station, who did not do better work and put forth greater effort under a spirit of approval than he would ever do under a spirit of criticism.　～ *Charles Schwab*

——— ARGUE ———

There's nothing so annoying as arguing with a person who knows what he is talking about.

Some arguments are sound, and nothing more.

～ *Richard Armour*

Arguing is a game that two can play at. But it is a strange game in that neither opponent ever wins.

～ *Benjamin Franklin*

If you argue and rankle and contradict, you may achieve a temporary victory—sometimes; but it will be an empty victory because you will never get your opponent's good will.　～ *Benjamin Franklin*

I always get the better when I argue alone.

～ *Oliver Goldsmith*

Never argue with a fool; people might not know the difference.

A dry crust eaten in peace is better than steak every day along with argument and strife.

～ *Proverbs 17:1*

—— ARMY ——

Any army of sheep led by a lion would defeat an army of lions led by a sheep.

~ Arab Proverb

—— ATHEIST ——

The worst moment for the atheist is when he is really thankful and has nobody to thank.

~ Dante Gabriel Rossetti

Did you hear about "Dial A Prayer" for atheists? You dial a number and no one answers.

I was going to be an atheist, but I gave it up. They don't have any holidays.

An atheist does not find God for the same reason a thief does not find a policeman.

—— ATTITUDE ——

Things are for us only what we hold them to be. Which is to say that our attitude toward things is more likely in the long run to be more important than the things themselves. *~ A.W. Tozer*

When a man is gloomy, everything seems to go wrong; when he is cheerful, everything seems right!

~ Proverbs 15:15

Perhaps the greatest discovery of this century is that if you can change your attitude, you can change your life. *~ William James*

Don't bother to give God instructions; just report for duty. *~ Corrie ten Boom*

Be like a duck—keep calm and unruffled on the surface, but paddle like crazy underneath.

Assume a cheerfulness you do not feel and shortly you will feel the cheerfulness you assumed. *~ Chinese Proverb*

I am more and more convinced that our happiness or unhappiness depends far more on the way we meet the events of life than on the nature of those events themselves. *~ Wilhelm von Humboldt*

If you want to sing, you will find a song.

A man is not hurt so much by what happens, as by his opinion of what happens. *~ Michel de Montaigne*

> To look up and not down,
> To look forward and not back,
> To look out and not in, and
> To lend a hand.
>
> *~ Edward Everett Hale*

He is a wise man who does not grieve for the things which he has not, but rejoices for those which he has.

~ *Epictetus*

Two men look out through the same bars;
One sees the mud, and one the stars....

~ *Frederick Langbridge*

When life gives you lemons, make lemonade.

Our life is what our thoughts make it.

~ *Marcus Aurelius*

Everyone must have felt that a cheerful friend is like a sunny day, which sheds its brightness on all around; and most of us can, as we choose, make of this world either a palace or a prison. ~ *Sir John Lubbock*

Any fact facing us is not as important as our attitude toward it, for that determines our success or failure. The way you think about a fact may defeat you before you ever do anything about it. You are overcome by the fact because you think you are.

~ *Norman Vincent Peale*

Keep your face to the sunshine and you cannot see the shadow. ~ *Helen Keller*

My center is giving way, my right is retreating. Situation excellent. I shall attack.

~ Ferdinand Foch

One man gets nothing but discord out of a piano; another gets harmony. No one claims the piano is at fault. Life is about the same. The discord is there, and the harmony is there. Study to play it correctly, and it will give forth the beauty; play it falsely, and it will give forth the ugliness. Life is not at fault.

If you wish to travel far and fast, travel light. Take off all your envies, jealousies, unforgiveness, selfishness and fears. *~ Glenn Clark*

In War: Resolution. In Defeat: Defiance. In Victory: Magnanimity. In Peace: Goodwill.

~ Winston Churchill

—— AUTHORITY ——

Nothing more impairs authority than a too frequent or indiscreet use of it. If thunder itself was to be continual, it would excite no more terror than the noise of a mill.

—— AUTOMOBILE ——

The worst kind of car trouble is when the engine won't start and the payments won't stop.

───── AVERAGE ─────

If at first you don't succeed, you're about average.
~ *Dr. Robert Anthony*

───── AVOIDANCE ─────

Things do not get better by being left alone. Unless they are adjusted, they explode with a shattering detonation. ~ *Winston Churchill*

───── BABIES ─────

Babies don't need a traditional slap on the rear end when they are born. But at least it gives them an immediate idea of what life is going to be like.

Out of the mouth of babes comes a lot of what they should have swallowed. ~ *Franklin P. Jones*

───── BAD ─────

There are bad people who would be less dangerous if they had no good in them.

~ *Francois
de La Rochefoucauld*

BALANCE

Things equal out pretty well. Our dreams seldom come true, but then neither do our nightmares.

~ *C. Kennedy*

BALD

When God made heads, he covered up the ones he didn't like.

BAR

The best side of a bar is outside.

BARBARIAN

History teaches us that when a barbarian race confronts a sleeping culture, the barbarian always wins.

~ *Arnold Toynbee*

BARGAIN

One of the difficult tasks in this world is to convince a woman that even a bargain costs money.

~ *Edgar Watson Howe*

BEANS

Abstain from beans.   ~ *Plutarch*

——— BEAUTY ———

Nothing is more beautiful than cheerfulness in an old face. ~*J.P. Richter*

Though we travel the world over to find the beautiful, we must carry it with us or we find it not.

~*Ralph Waldo Emerson*

There is no cosmetic for beauty like happiness.

~*Lady Blessington*

A thing of beauty is a joy forever.

~*John Keats*

——— BED ———

No bed is big enough to hold three.

~*German Proverb*

——— BEHAVIOR ———

Be pleasant until ten o'clock in the morning and the rest of the day will take care of itself.

~*Elbert Hubbard*

As I grow older, I pay less attention to what men say. I just watch what they do.   ~*Andrew Carnegie*

——— BELIEF ———

Whether you believe you can do a thing or not, you are right.   ~*Henry Ford*

What we believe about God is the most important thing about us.   ~*A.W. Tozer*

Believe only half of what you see and nothing that you hear.   ~*Dinah Mulock Craik*

It is so hard to believe because it is so hard to obey.

~*Soren Kierkegaard*

——— BELITTLE ———

You can't hold a man down without staying down with him.   ~*Booker T. Washington*

——— BENEFIT ———

He who receives a benefit should never forget it; he who bestows one should never remember it.

~*Pierre Charron*

BEWARE

Beware equally of a sudden friend, and a slow enemy. ~*John Home*

Beware of the little expenses; a small leak will sink a great ship. ~*Benjamin Franklin*

A man should be careful never to tell tales of himself to his own disadvantage; people may be amused, and laugh at the time, but they will be remembered, and brought up against him upon some subsequent occasion. ~*Samuel Johnson*

BIBLE

When you have read the Bible, you will know it is the Word of God, because you will have found it the key to your own heart, your own happiness, and your own duty. ~*Woodrow Wilson*

A knowledge of the Bible without a college degree is far more valuable than a college degree without the knowledge of the Bible. ~*William Lyon Phelps*

The Scriptures teach us the best way of living, the noblest way of suffering, and the most comfortable way of dying. ~*John Flavel*

Men do not reject the Bible because it contradicts itself but because it contradicts them.

~*E. Paul Hovey*

If a man's Bible is coming apart, it is an indication that he himself is fairly well put together.

~ *James Jennings*

Why is it that our kids can't read a Bible in school, but they can in prison?

The Bible will keep you from sin, or sin will keep you from the Bible. ~ *D.L. Moody*

It ain't those parts of the Bible that I can't understand that bother me, it is the parts that I do understand. ~ *Mark Twain*

When Thomas Paine showed Benjamin Franklin the manuscript of *The Age of Reason*, Franklin advised him not to publish it, saying, "The world is bad enough with the Bible; what would it be without it?"

~ *Anonymous*

 **BIRD**

A bird in the hand is worth two in the bush.

~ *Cervantes*

Birds of a feather will flock together.

~ *Minsheu*

——— BIRTH ———

This day shall change all griefs and quarrels into love. *~ William Shakespeare*

The only time a woman wishes she were a year older is when she is expecting a baby.

~ Mary Marsh

——— BITTERNESS ———

Bitterness and resentment are conditions of the heart which develop because a person allows an offense or disappointment to take root and grow until it affects his thoughts, actions, and his interpersonal relationships. *~ Billy Graham*

——— BLAME ———

The only person who cannot be helped is that person who blames another. *~ Carl Rogers*

The quickest way to take the starch out of a fellow who is always blaming himself is to agree with him.

~ Josh Billings

To err is human. To blame it on the other guy is even more human. *~ Bits and Pieces*

—— BLESSING ——

Blessings never come in pairs; misfortunes never come alone.　　　*~Chinese Proverb*

If it is more blessed to give than to receive, then most of us are content to let the other fellow have the greater blessing.　　　*~Shailer Mathews*

—— BLIND ——

There's none so blind as they that won't see.
　　　~Jonathan Swift

—— BLUFF ——

The hardest tumble a man can make is to fall over his own bluff.　　　*~Ambrose Bierce*

—— BLUNTNESS ——

If you say what you think, don't expect to hear only what you like.　　　*~Malcolm Forbes*

—— BOAST ——

Great boaster, little doer.

—— **BOOK** ——

A book is the only place in which you can examine a fragile thought without breaking it, or explore an explosive idea without fear it will go off in your face.... It is one of the few havens remaining where a man's mind can get both provocation and privacy.

~ *Edward P. Morgan*

There's no thief like a bad book.

~ *Italian Proverb*

In every fat book there is a thin book trying to get out.

This book fills a much-needed gap.

~ *Moses Hadas*

'Tis pleasant, sure, to see one's name in print;
A book's a book, although there's nothing in't.

~ *Lord Byron*

Books serve to show a man that those original thoughts of his aren't very new after all.

~ *Abraham Lincoln*

There is more treasure in books than in all the pirates' loot on Treasure Island ... and best of all, you can enjoy these riches every day of your life.

~ *Walt Disney*

The man who doesn't read good books has no advantage over the man who can't read them.

~ *Mark Twain*

When I get a little money, I buy books; and if any is left, I buy food and clothes.

~ *Desiderius Erasmus*

The books I haven't written are better than the books other people have.   ~ *Cyril V. Connolly*

Someday I hope to write a book where the royalties will pay for the copies I give away.

~ *Clarence Darrow*

No furniture so charming as books, even if you never open them, or read a single word.

~ *Sydney Smith*

I hate having new books forced upon me, but how I love cram-throating other people with them.

~ *Logan Pearsall Smith*

The books that everybody admires are those that nobody reads.   ~ *Anatole France*

—— BORE ——

The secret of being a bore is to tell everything.

~ *Voltaire*

A bore is a fellow talker who can change the subject to his topic of conversation faster than you can change it back to yours.   ~ *Laurence J. Peter*

Bores can be divided into two classes: those who have their own particular subject, and those who do not need a subject.   ~ *A.A. Milne*

We often boast that we are never bored, but yet we are so conceited that we do not perceive how often we bore others.   ~ *Francois*
de La Rochefoucauld

―――― **BOREDOM** ――――

Millions long for immortality who do not know what to do with themselves on a rainy Sunday afternoon.   ~ *Susan Ertz*

It is not the fast tempo of modern life that kills but the boredom, a lack of strong interest, and a failure to grow that destroy. It is the feeling that nothing is worthwhile that makes men ill and unhappy.

~ *Harold Dodds*

The most bored people in life are not the under-privileged but the overprivileged.

~ *Fulton Sheen*

Boredom is the root of all evil—the despairing refusal to be oneself. *~ Soren Kierkegaard*

I spent a year in that town, one Sunday.

~ Warwick Deeping

——— BORROWING ———

He that goes a borrowing goes a sorrowing.

——— BOSS ———

The question, "Who ought to be boss?" is like asking "Who ought to be the tenor in the quartet?" Obviously, the man who can sing tenor.

~ Henry Ford

——— BOWELS ———

I have finally come to the conclusion that a good reliable set of bowels is worth more to a man than any quantity of brains. *~ Josh Billings*

——— BRAGGING ———

Nobody's so apt to be a soloist as the fellow who blows his own horn. *~ Franklin P. Jones*

—— BRAIN ——

The brain is a wonderful organ; it starts working the moment you get up in the morning and does not stop until you get to the office.

~ *Robert Frost*

What's on your mind? If you will forgive the over-statement.　　　　~ *Fred Allen*

—— BRAVERY ——

Bravery is being the only one who knows you're afraid.　　　　~ *Franklin P. Jones*

If you are brave too often, people will come to expect it of you.　　　　~ *Mignon McLaughlin*

It is easy to be brave from a safe distance.

~ *Aesop*

Bravery is the capacity to perform properly even when scared half to death.　　~ *General Omar Bradley*

—— BREEDING ——

Men are generally more careful of the breed of their horses and dogs than of their children.

~ *William Penn*

BREVITY

It is when I am struggling to be brief that I become unintelligible.　　*~Horace*

BRIDE

The weeping bride makes a laughing wife.

BROKENNESS

A cheerful heart does good like medicine, but a broken spirit makes one sick.

~Proverbs 17:22

A man's courage can sustain his broken body, but when courage dies, what hope is left?

~Proverbs 18:14

BURDENS

It has been well said that no man ever sank under the burden of the day. It is when tomorrow's burden is added to the burden of today that the weight is more than a man can bear.　　*~George MacDonald*

No one is useless in this world who lightens the burdens of another.   ~ *Charles Dickens*

——— BUSINESS ———

An empty stable stays clean—but there is no income from an empty stable.   ~ *Proverbs 14:4*

Any enterprise is built by wise planning, becomes strong through common sense, and profits wonderfully by keeping abreast of the facts.

~ *Proverbs 24:3, 4*

Develop your business first before building your house.   ~ *Proverbs 24:27*

Let the buyer beware.   ~ *Latin Maxim*

Business is like a wheelbarrow—it stands still until someone pushes it.

——— CALAMITY ———

Calamities are of two kinds: misfortune to ourselves, and good fortune to others.

~ *Ambrose Bierce*

CAPITALISM

The inherent vice of capitalism is the unequal sharing of blessings; the inherent vice of socialism is the equal sharing of miseries.

~ Winston Churchill

CAR

Any car will last a lifetime, if you're careless enough.

CARE

A good manager is a man who isn't worried about his own career but rather the careers of those who work for him. My advice: Don't worry about yourself. Take care of those who work for you and you'll float to greatness on their achievements.

~ H.M.S. Burns

Nobody cares how much you know—until they know how much you care.   *~ John Cassis*

To carry care to bed is to sleep with a pack on your back.   *~ T.C. Haliburton*

CARELESSNESS

For want of a nail the shoe was lost; for want of a shoe the horse was lost; and for the want of a horse the rider was lost; being overtaken and slain by the enemy, all for want of care about a horseshoe nail.

~ *Benjamin Franklin*

CARES

The night shall be filled with music
And the cares that infest the day
Shall fold their tents like the Arabs,
And silently steal away.

~ *Henry Wadsworth
Longfellow*

CARPENTER

By a Carpenter mankind was made, and only by that Carpenter can mankind be remade.

~ *Desiderius Erasmus*

CATS

No matter how much cats fight, there always seem to be plenty of kittens. ~ *Abraham Lincoln*

When the cat's away the mice will play.

~ *English Proverb*

CAUTION

It is a good thing to learn caution by the misfortunes of others. ~ *Publilius Syrus*

Just because the river is quiet, don't think the crocodiles have left. ~ *Malay Proverb*

A wise man does not trust all his eggs to one basket.

~ *Cervantes*

Little boats should keep near shore.

~ *Benjamin Franklin*

Be on your guard against a silent dog and still water.

~ *Latin Proverb*

There's always free cheese in a mousetrap.

CELEBRITY

A celebrity is a person who works hard all his life to become well known, and then wears dark glasses to avoid being recognized. ~ *Fred Allen*

CHALLENGE

Challenge causes one to rise to the occasion and put forth his best abilities to overcome obstacles and pressures and grow in character.

Do the hard jobs first. The easy jobs will take care of themselves. ~ *Dale Carnegie*

——— CHANGE ———

All change represents loss of some kind; that's why some of us resist it so strongly.

Consider how hard it is to change yourself and you'll understand what little chance you have of trying to change others. ~ *Jacob M. Braude*

Change is always hard for the man who is in a rut. For he has scaled down his living to that which he can handle comfortably and welcomes no change—or challenge— that would lift him. ~ *C. Neil Strait*

The world hates change; yet it is the only thing that has brought progress. ~ *Charles F. Kettering*

——— CHARACTER ———

Ability will enable a man to get to the top, but it takes character to keep him there.

If I keep my good character, I shall be rich enough. ~ *Platonicus*

A person reveals his character by nothing so clearly as the joke he resents. ~ *G.C. Lichtenberg*

Every man has three characters—that which he exhibits, that which he has, and that which he thinks he has. ~ *Alphonse Karr*

Some men work hard and save money so their sons won't have the problems that made men of their fathers.

You can tell a company by the men it keeps.

~ W.A. Clarke

A man can be no bigger than the number of people for whom he genuinely cares.

~ Sherm Williams

Character is what you are in the dark.

~ D.L. Moody

The way to find out about one man, I have often found, is to ask him about another.

~ Gerard Fay

You cannot help men permanently by doing for them what they could and should do for themselves.

~ Abraham Lincoln

The surest way to make it hard for your children is to make it soft for them.

It is not a question of how much a man knows, but of the use he makes of what he knows; not a question of what he has acquired, and how he has been trained, but of what he is and what he can do.

~ Josiah G. Holland

A man's reputation is only what men think him to be; his character is what God knows him to be.

I never knew an early-rising, hard-working, prudent man, careful of his earnings, and strictly honest, who complained of bad luck. A good character, good habits, and iron industry are impregnable to the assaults of all the ill luck that fools ever dreamed of.

~Joseph Addison

A pat on the back develops character, if it is administered young enough, often enough, and low enough.

I am only one, but I am one. I can't do everything, but I can do something. And what I can do, that I ought to do. And what I ought to do, by the grace of God, I shall do. *~Edward E. Hale*

——— CHARM ———

There's a difference between beauty and charm. A beautiful woman is one I notice. A charming woman is one who notices me. *~John Erskine*

——— CHEAT ———

He who will cheat you at play will cheat you in other ways.

CHEER

The best way to cheer yourself is to try to cheer somebody else. ~*Megiddo Message*

He who sings frightens away his ills.
~*Cervantes*

A cheerful look makes a dish a feast.
~*George Herbert*

Let us be of good cheer, remembering that the misfortunes hardest to bear are those which never happen. ~*Lowell*

A good laugh is sunshine in a house.
~*William M. Thackeray*

CHILD

How sharper than a serpent's tooth it is to have a thankless child. ~*William Shakespeare*

CHILDHOOD

Teach your child to hold his tongue; he'll learn fast enough to speak. ~*Benjamin Franklin*

The wildest colts make the best horses.
~*Plutarch*

It is a wise father that knows his own child.

~ *William Shakespeare*

The best way to make children good is to make them happy. ~ *Oscar Wilde*

———— CHILDREN ————

When I approach a child, he inspires in me two sentiments: tenderness for what he is, and a respect for what he may become. ~ *Louis Pasteur*

Teach a child to choose the right path, and when he is older he will remain upon it.

~ *Proverbs 22:6*

The persons hardest to convince they're at the retirement age are children at bedtime.

~ *Shannon Fife*

The thing that impresses me most about America is the way parents obey their children.

~ *Duke of Windsor*

As the twig is bent the tree inclines.

~ *Virgil*

You can do anything with children if you only play with them. ~ *Prince Otto von Bismarck*

There was never a child so lovely but his mother was glad to get him asleep.   *~ Ralph Waldo Emerson*

No wonder kids are confused today. Half of the adults tell them to find themselves; the other half tell them to get lost.

Children are like mosquitoes—the moment they stop making noises you know they're getting into something.

Kids really brighten a household. They never turn off any lights.   *~ Ralph Bus*

Children are a real comfort in your old age—the problem is that they make you reach it sooner.

Oh, what a tangled web we weave when first we practice to conceive.   *~ Don Herold*

Children begin by loving their parents; as they grow older they judge them; sometimes they forgive them.   *~ Oscar Wilde*

Kids used to ask where they came from; now they tell you where to go.

—— **CHOICE** ——

He who does not make a choice makes a choice.

——— CHRIST ———

Alexander, Caesar, Charlemagne, and I myself have founded empires; but upon what do these creations of our genius depend? Upon force. Jesus alone founded his empire upon love; and to this very day millions would die for him.

~Napoleon

——— CHRISTIAN ———

The Christian's chief occupational hazards are depression and discouragement.

~John Stott

Too many Christians want to reach the promised land without going through the wilderness.

Whatever makes men good Christians makes them good citizens.   *~Daniel Webster*

A man ought to live so that everybody knows he is a Christian...and most of all, his family ought to know.

~D.L. Moody

——— CHRISTIANITY ———

Christianity has not been tried and found wanting; it has been found difficult and not tried.

~G.K. Chesterton

—— **CHRISTMAS** ——

Shopping in crowded stores gives me Santa Claustrophobia.

For the millions who have been saving for a rainy day, Christmas is the monsoon season.

~ *Thinking Out Loud*

—— **CHURCH** ——

Division has done more to hide Christ from the view of men than all the infidelity that has ever been spoken.

~ *George MacDonald*

Where God has his church, the Devil will have his chapel. ~ *Spanish Proverb*

Though the church has many critics, it has no rivals.

—— **CIRCUMSTANCES** ——

People are always blaming their circumstances for what they are. I don't believe in circumstances. The people who get on in this world are the people who get up and look for the circumstances they want, and, if they can't find them, make them.

~ *George Bernard Shaw*

——— CLASSIC ———

Classic: A book which people praise and don't read.

~ *Mark Twain*

——— CLEVERNESS ———

What makes us so bitter against people who outwit us is that they think themselves cleverer than we are.

~ *Francois
de La Rochefoucauld*

It takes much cleverness to know how to conceal cleverness.

~ *Francois
de La Rochefoucauld*

——— CLOTHES ———

Freedom of the press means no-iron clothes.

It is an interesting question how far men would retain their relative rank if they were divested of their clothes.

~ *Henry David Thoreau*

——— COLD ———

A cold is both positive and negative; sometimes the Eyes have it and sometimes the Nose.

~ *William Lyon Phelps*

COLLEGE

You can lead a boy to college but you cannot make him think. *~ Elbert Hubbard*

COMEDY

Tragedy plus time equals comedy.

~ Steve Allen

COMMAND

Those who can command themselves, command others. *~ William Hazlitt*

COMMITMENT

Commitment: The ability to bind oneself emotionally and intellectually to a idea or task that needs to be completed.

COMMITTEE

You'll never find in no park or city, a monument to a committee. *~ Victoria Pasternak*

Committee: A group of men who keep minutes and waste hours. *~ Milton Berle*

The larger the number of people involved in any given decision, the greater the pressure for conformity.   ~ *Psychology Today*

A conference is a gathering of important people who singly can do nothing, but together can decide that nothing can be done.   ~ *Fred Allen*

——— **COMMON** ———

God must love the common man, he made so many of them.   ~ *Abraham Lincoln*

——— **COMMON SENSE** ———

Common sense is the knack of seeing things as they are, and doing things as they ought to be done.

——— **COMMUNICATION** ———

Half of the world's problems are caused by poor communications. The other half are caused by good communications.

——— **COMMUNISM** ———

Communism is a religion and only as we see it as a religion, though a secular religion, will we understand its power.   ~ *Elton Trueblood*

COMPANIONS

Birds of a feather will gather together.

~ Robert Burton

One crow will not pick out another crow's eyes.

~ English Proverb

He who lies down with the dogs will get up with the fleas.

Associate with men of good quality, if you esteem your own reputation; for it is better to be alone than in bad company. *~ George Washington*

COMPLAIN

When I complain, I do it because "it's good to get things off my chest"; when you complain, I remind you that "griping doesn't help anything."

~ Sydney Harris

I had no shoes and complained until I met a man who had no feet.

Some people seem to go through life standing at the complaint counter. *~ Fred Propp, Jr.*

A constant dripping on a rainy day and a cranky woman are much alike! You can no more stop her complaints than you can stop the wind or hold onto anything with oil-slick hands.

~ *Proverbs 27:15, 16*

COMPLETION

There is nothing more invigorating than the knowledge of tasks efficiently completed and there is nothing more dispiriting than the knowledge of unfulfilled responsibilities.   ~ *John Haggai*

COMPLIMENT

I can live for two months on a good compliment.

~ *Mark Twain*

Some people pay a compliment as if they expected a receipt.   ~ *Frank Hubbard*

COMPOSE

In order to compose, all you need to do is remember a tune that nobody else has thought of.

~ *Robert Schumann*

––––––– **CONCEIT** –––––––

Wind puffs up empty bladders: opinions and fools.

~ *Socrates*

There is one thing worse than a fool, and that is a man who is conceited.   ~ *Proverbs 26:12*

No man was ever so much deceived by another as by himself.   ~ *Greville*

Conceit causes more conversation than wit.

~ *Francois
de La Rochefoucauld*

––––––– **CONCENTRATION** –––––––

One great cause of failure of young men in business is the lack of concentration. ~ *Andrew Carnegie*

––––––– **CONCERN** –––––––

When I have something that causes me concern, I just dismiss everything connected with it from my mind and let my work absorb me. It's surprising how it clears up.

——— CONCILIATION ———

An infallible method of conciliating a tiger is to allow oneself to be devoured.

~ *Konrad Adenauer*

——— CONFESSION ———

Confessions may be good for the soul but they are bad for the reputation.   ~ *Thomas Dewar*

——— CONFLICT ———

Conflict can be an opportunity for growth or the tool for destruction of relationships.

——— CONFUSE ———

If you can't convince them, confuse them.

~ *Harry S. Truman*

——— CONFUSION ———

The battle of the sexes will have to be called off, if it gets any harder for one side to identify the other.

~ *Franklin P. Jones*

——— CONGESTION ———

The thing which in the subway is called congestion is highly esteemed in the night spots as intimacy.

~ *Simeon Strunsky*

——— CONGRESS ———

There are two periods when Congress does no business: one is before holidays, and the other after.

~ *George Prentice*

With Congress, every time they make a joke it's a law; and every time they make a law it's a joke.

~ *Will Rogers*

Reader, suppose you were an idiot; and suppose you were a member of Congress; but I repeat myself.

~ *Mark Twain*

——— CONQUEROR ———

He is the greatest conqueror who has conquered himself.

——— CONSCIENCE ———

A good conscience is a soft pillow.

Harken to the warnings of conscience, if you would not feel its wounds.

I value people with a conscience. It's like a beeper from God. ~ *Robert Orben*

There's no substitute for conscience. Unless, of course, it's witnesses. ~ *Franklin P. Jones*

There is no better tranquilizer than a clear conscience.

He who has a good conscience has a continual Christmas.

I am more afraid of my own heart than of the pope and all his cardinals. I have within me the great pope, self. ~ *Martin Luther*

Conscience: The inner voice which warns us that someone may be looking. ~ *H.L. Mencken*

––––––– **CONSISTENCY** –––––––

Consistency requires you to be as ignorant today as you were a year ago. ~ *Bernard Berenson*

––––––– **CONTEMPT** –––––––

Perhaps the greatest sin one person can exert against another is contempt. To exercise contempt is to invite contempt. Any person who looks with contempt upon another sets in motion an evil force which rarely ever stops. ~ *Charles Ashcraft*

———— CONTENTMENT ————

After all, we didn't bring any money with us when we came into the world, and we can't carry away a single penny when we die. So we should be well satisfied without money if we have enough food and clothing. ~ *1 Timothy 6:7, 8*

Contentment comes not so much from great wealth as from few wants. ~ *Epictetus*

True contentment is the power of getting out of any situation all that there is in it.

~ *G.K. Chesterton*

My crown is in my heart, not on my head;
Not deck'd with diamonds and Indian stones,
Nor to be seen: my crown is called content;
A crown it is that seldom kings enjoy.

~ *William Shakespeare*

The secret of contentment is knowing how to enjoy what you have, and to be able to lose all desire for things beyond your reach. ~ *Lin Yutang*

———— CONTROVERSY ————

When a thing ceases to be a subject of controversy, it ceases to be a subject of interest.

~ *William Hazlitt*

———— CONVERSATION ————

If you think before you speak, the other fellow gets in his joke first. *~Ed Howe*

No man would listen to you talk if he didn't know it was his turn next. *~Ed Howe*

Think twice before you speak—and you'll find everyone talking about something else.

~ Francis Kitman

One of the reasons that we find so few persons rational and agreeable in conversation is that there is hardly a person who does not think more of what he wants to say than of his answer to what is said.

*~ Francois
de La Rochefoucauld*

The more clever and polite think it enough simply to put on an attentive expression, while all the time you can see in their eyes and train of thought that they are far removed from what you are saying, and are anxious to get back to what they want to say. They ought, on the contrary, to reflect that such keenness to please oneself is a bad way of pleasing or persuading others, and that to listen well and answer to the point is one of the most perfect qualities one can have in conversation. *~ Francois
de La Rochefoucauld*

One secret of successful conversation is learning to disagree without being disagreeable. It isn't what, but how you speak that makes all the difference. Ben Franklin used to remark diplomatically, "On this point, I agree. But on the other, if you don't mind, may I take exception."   *~ Jack Harrison Pollack*

For good or ill, your conversation is your advertisement. Every time you open your mouth you let men look into your mind.   *~ Bruce Barton*

The less men think, the more they talk.

~Charles de Montesquieu

A single conversation with a wise man is better than ten years of study.   *~ Chinese Proverb*

Conversation is a serious matter. There are men with whom an hour's talk would weaken one more than a week's fasting.   *~ English Proverb*

——— CONVICTIONS ———

Beware lest we mistake our prejudices for our convictions.   *~ Harry A. Ironside*

There are ten church members by inheritance for one by conviction.   *~ Austin O'Malley*

——— COOKING ———

God sends meat—the Devil sends cooks.

~ Charles VI

A practical cookbook is one that has a blank page in the back—where you list the numbers of the nearest delicatessen.

——— COOPERATION ———

You cannot sink someone else's end of the boat and still keep your own afloat.   ~*Charles Brower*

——— CORRUPT ———

The more corrupt the state, the more numerous the laws.   ~*Tacitus*

The greater the number of laws and enactments, the more thieves and robbers there will be.

~*Lao-Tzu*

——— COUNSEL ———

Without wise leadership, a nation is in trouble; but with good counselors there is safety.

~*Proverbs 11:14*

Plans go wrong with too few counselors; many counselors bring success.   ~*Proverbs 15:22*

——— COURAGE ———

Far better it is to dare mighty things, to win glorious triumphs, even though checkered by failure, than to take rank with those poor spirits who neither enjoy much nor suffer much, because they live in the gray twilight that knows not victory or defeat.

~ Theodore Roosevelt

Often the test of courage is not to die but to live.

~ Conte Vittorio Alfieri

Courage is the mastery of fear, not the absence of fear. *~ Mark Twain*

Courage is doing what you're afraid to do. There can be no courage unless you're scared.

~ Eddie Rickenbacker

Courage comes by being brave; fear comes by holding back. *~ Publilius Syrus*

He that loses money loses little, he that loses health loses much, but he that loses courage loses all.

Courage is rightly esteemed the first of human qualities because it is the quality which guarantees all others. *~ Winston Churchill*

If you want to develop courage, do the thing you fear to do and keep on doing it until you get a record of successful experiences behind you. That is the quickest and surest way ever yet discovered to conquer fear.

~ Dale Carnegie

COURT

Don't be hot-headed and rush to court! You may start something you can't finish and go down before your neighbor in shameful defeat. So discuss the matter with him privately. Don't tell anyone else, lest he accuse you of slander and you can't withdraw what you said. *~ Proverbs 25:8-10*

COURTESY

Practice courtesy. You never know when it might become popular again. *~ Bill Copeland*

Nothing is more becoming in a great man than courtesy and forbearance. *~ Cicero*

Life is not so short but that there is always time enough for courtesy. *~ Ralph Waldo Emerson*

COURTING

He who would the daughter win, must with the mother first begin.

COVETOUSNESS

The man who covets is always poor.
~ Claudian

─────── **COWARDICE** ───────

To sin by silence when they should protest makes cowards out of men.   *~ Abraham Lincoln*

Cowards die many times before their deaths; the valiant never taste of death but once.

~ William Shakespeare

─────── **CRABBY** ───────

It is better to live in the corner of an attic than with a crabby woman in a lovely home.

~ Proverbs 21:9

─────── **CRANKY** ───────

It is better to live in a corner of an attic than in a beautiful home with a cranky, quarrelsome woman.

~ Proverbs 25:24

─────── **CRAZY** ───────

One out of four people in this country is mentally imbalanced. Think of your three closest friends. If they seem okay, then you're the one.

~ Ann Landers

—— CREATIVITY ——

No matter how old you get, if you can keep the desire to be creative, you're keeping the man-child alive.   ~ *John Cassavetes*

Creative minds always have been known to survive any kind of bad training.   ~ *Anna Freud*

Creative minds are rarely tidy.

In my experience, the best creative work is never done when one is unhappy. ~ *Albert Einstein*

Creativity is so delicate a flower that praise tends to make it bloom, while discouragement often nips it in the bud. Any of us will put out more and better ideas if our efforts are truly appreciated.

~ *Alexander Osborn*

Creativity is essentially a lonely art. An even lonelier struggle. To some a blessing. To others a curse. It is in reality the ability to reach inside yourself and drag forth from your very soul an idea.

~ *Lou Dorfsman*

Teamwork may be good for morale, but when new ideas are needed, it's best to let people work on their own. Research shows that people who were left by themselves to think about subjects they considered relevant came up with three times as many ideas as those who brainstormed in groups. Researchers believe that when people work in groups, their creativity is inhibited by fear of criticism and real or perceived pressures to conform.   ~ *Horizons*

You cannot order people to be creative. People are creative only when they are doing the things they want to do.   ~ *Herman Krannert*

CREDIBILITY

Do what is expected of you and you gain credibility. Don't do what is expected of you and you lose credibility.

CREDIT CARDS

The surest way to establish your credit is to work yourself into the position of not needing any.

CRIME

One crime is concealed by the commission of another.   ~ *Seneca*

Save a thief from the gallows and he will be the first to cut your throat.   ~ *Italian Proverb*

Most people fancy themselves innocent of those crimes of which they cannot be convicted.

~ *Seneca*

—— CRISIS ——

The nearer any disease approaches to a crisis, the nearer it is to a cure. Danger and deliverance make their advances together; and it is only in the last push that one or the other takes the lead.

~ *Thomas Paine*

—— CRITIC ——

The writers against religion, whilst they oppose every system, are wisely careful never to set up any of their own. ~ *Edmund Burke*

A critic is a legless man who teaches running.

~ *Channing Pollock*

Pay no attention to what the critics say; there has never been set up a statue in honor of a critic.

~ *Jean Sibelius*

Those who have free seats at a play hiss first.

~ *Chinese Proverb*

It is easier to pull down than to build up.

~ *Latin Proverb*

If what they are saying about you is true, mend your ways. If it isn't true, forget it, and go on and serve the Lord. ~ *Harry A. Ironside*

It is a badge of honor to accept valid criticism.

~ *Proverbs 25:12*

Criticism is a study by which men grow important and formidable at very small expense.

~ *Samuel Johnson*

To escape criticism—do nothing, say nothing, be nothing. ~ *Elbert Hubbard*

Criticism comes easier than craftsmanship.

~ *Zeuxis*

I have read your lousy review of Margaret's concert. I've come to the conclusion that you are "an eight ulcer man on four ulcer pay." Some day I hope to meet you. When that happens you'll need a new nose, a lot of beefsteak for black eyes, and perhaps a supporter below. ~ *Harry S. Truman*

Honest criticism is hard to take, particularly from a relative, a friend, an acquaintance, or a stranger.

~ *Franklin P. Jones*

Tall trees catch much wind.

He has a right to criticize who has a heart to help.

~ *Abraham Lincoln*

No one so thoroughly appreciates the value of constructive criticism as the one who's giving it.

~ *Hal Chadwick*

If you are not big enough to stand criticism, you are too small to be praised.   ~ *Grit*

If you would be loved as a companion, avoid unnecessary criticisms of those with whom you live.

~ *Arthur Helps*

What people say about us is never quite true; but it is never quite false, either; they always miss the bull's-eye, but they rarely fail to hit the target.

~ *Sydney Harris*

Even the lion has to defend himself against flies.

~ *German Proverb*

If I were to try to read, much less to answer, all the attacks made on me, this shop might as well be closed for any other business. I do the very best I know how—the very best I can; and I mean to keep on doing so until the end. If the end brings me out all right, then what is said against me won't matter. If the end brings me out wrong, then ten angels swearing I was right would make no difference.   ~ *Abraham Lincoln*

Criticize by creating.   ~ *Michelangelo*

It was one of those plays in which the actors unfortunately enunciated very clearly.

~ *Robert Benchley*

No one ever kicks a dead dog.

If you get kicked from behind, it is because you are out in front. ~ *R.E. Phillips*

Any fool can criticize, condemn, and complain—and most fools do. ~ *Benjamin Franklin*

There are three reasons why people criticize. First, we criticize in order to elevate ourselves. Second, we criticize in order to project our miserableness. Third, we criticize the very thing of which we are guilty, or the thing which tempts us and troubles us the most.

~ *John Haggai*

—— CROOK ——

In all my years of public life I have never obstructed justice.... Your President is no crook!

~ *Richard M. Nixon*

—— CROWN ——

Uneasy lies the head that wears a crown.

~ *William Shakespeare*

—— **CRUCIFY** ——

We crucify ourselves between two thieves; regret for yesterday and fear of tomorrow.

~ *Fulton Oursler*

—— **CRUELTY** ——

All cruelty springs from weakness.

~ *Seneca*

—— **CURIOSITY** ——

Life can be one dreary day after another or a Bagdad of fascinating things to keep learning. Get more out of every phase of your life—stay incurably curious.

~ *L. Perry Wilbur*

A bright eye indicates curiosity; a black eye, too much.   ~ *Sunshine*

Curiosity killed the cat.   ~ *American Proverb*

—— **CURSE** ——

If you shout a pleasant greeting to a friend too early in the morning, he will count it as a curse!

~ *Proverbs 27:14*

DANGER

Wherever there is danger, there lurks opportunity; whenever there is opportunity there lurks danger. The two are inseparable; they go together.

~ *Earl Nightingale*

DAY

This is the day which the Lord hath made; we will rejoice and be glad in it.   ~ *Psalm 118:24 (KJV)*

DEATH

Man weeps to think that he will die so soon; woman, that she was born so long ago.

~ *H.L. Mencken*

I never wanted to see anybody die, but there are a few obituary notices I have read with pleasure.

~ *Clarence Darrow*

The beginnings and endings of all human undertakings are untidy.   ~ *John Galsworthy*

I'm not afraid to die. I just don't want to be there when it happens.   ~ *Woody Allen*

I hate death; in fact, I could live forever without it.

~ *Pogo*

My grandfather would look through the obituary columns and say to me, "Strange, isn't it, how everybody seems to die in alphabetical order."

~ Jackie Vernon

Death: To stop sinning suddenly.

~ Elbert Hubbard

——— **DEBT** ———

Pay all your debts except the debt of love for others—never finish paying that!

~ Romans 13:8

——— **DECEPTION** ———

We often shed tears which deceive ourselves after deceiving others. *~ Francois de La Rochefoucauld*

We are inclined to believe those we do not know, because they have never deceived us.

~ Samuel Johnson

Of all the agonies of life, that which is most poignant and harrowing—that which for the time annihilates reason and leaves our whole organization one lacerated, mangled heart—is the conviction that we have been deceived where we placed all the trust of love. *~ Bulwer*

No man was ever so much deceived by another as by himself.   *~ Greville*

You can fool some of the people all of the time, and all of the people some of the time, but you cannot fool all of the people all the time.

~ Abraham Lincoln

——— DECISION ———

Not to decide is to decide.

~ Harvey Cox

Decision is a sharp knife that cuts clean and straight; indecision is a dull one that hacks and tears and leaves ragged edges behind it.   *~ Gordon Graham*

When once a decision is reached and execution is the order of the day, dismiss absolutely all responsibility and care about the outcome.

Decide promptly, but never give any reasons. Your decisions may be right, but your reasons are sure to be wrong.   *~ Lord Mansfield*

Before you start looking for a peg, decide what hole you want to fill.

Once the facts are clear, the decisions jump out at you.
~ *Peter Drucker*

——— DEDICATION ———

Attempt great things for God and expect great things from God.
~ *William Carey*

——— DEED ———

Don't take the will for the deed; get the deed.
~ *Ethel Watts Mumford*

——— DEEDS ———

Good words without deeds are rushes and reeds.

——— DEFEAT ———

It's not the giants who defeat us, but the mosquitoes.
~ *Gage Spindler*

A defeat may be a victory in disguise.

It is defeat that turns bones to flint; it is defeat that turns gristle to muscle; it is defeat that makes men invincible.
~ *Henry Ward Beecher*

What is defeat? Nothing but education, nothing but the first step to something better.

DEFECTS

If we had no defects ourselves, we should not take so much pleasure in noting those of others.

> ~ *Francois*
> *de La Rochefoucauld*

DEMOCRACY

Man's capacity for justice makes democracy possible; but man's inclination to injustice makes democracy necessary.

DEMOCRATS

If the Republicans will stop telling lies about the Democrats, we will stop telling the truth about them.

> ~ *Adlai Stevenson*

DEPENDABILITY

The bottom line of dependability is, can you be trusted?
> ~ *R.E. Phillips*

A good horse never lacks a saddle.

—— DEPRESSION ——

One of the bad things about depression is that it drains us emotionally and makes us unable to handle things that normally would not get us down.

~ *Billy Graham*

—— DESIRE ——

If the desire to kill and the opportunity to kill came always together, who would escape hanging?

~ *Mark Twain*

Life contains but two tragedies. One is not to get your heart's desire; the other is to get it.

~ *Socrates*

—— DESPERATION ——

The mass of men lead lives of quiet desperation.

~ *Henry David Thoreau*

—— DESTINY ——

Lots of folks confuse bad management with destiny.

~ *Kin Hubbard*

DETAILS

It is the little bits of things that fret and worry us; we can dodge an elephant, but we can't a fly.

~ *Josh Billings*

DETERMINATION

Do what you can, with what you have, where you are.

~ *Theodore Roosevelt*

Our greatest glory is not in never falling, but in rising every time we fall.   ~ *Confucius*

When you get into a tight place and everything goes against you, till it seems as though you could not hold on a minute longer, never give up then, for that is just the place and time that the tide will turn.

~ *Harriet Beecher Stowe*

The men who try to do something and fail are infinitely better than those who try to do nothing and succeed.   ~ *Lloyd Jones*

I was the son of an immigrant. I experienced bigotry, intolerance, and prejudice, even as so many of you have. Instead of allowing these things to embitter me, I took them as spurs to more strenuous effort.

Not everything that is faced can be changed, but nothing can be changed until it is faced.

~ *James Baldwin*

Pray to God, but keep rowing to the shore.

~ *Russian Proverb*

If we all did the things we are capable of doing, we would literally astound ourselves.

~ *Thomas Edison*

No farmer ever plowed a field by turning it over in his mind.

—— DEVIL ——

The devil can quote scripture for his purpose.

~ *William Shakespeare*

The devil is a better theologian than any of us and is a devil still.   ~ *A.W. Tozer*

—— DIAMOND ——

It is better to have old secondhand diamonds than none at all.   ~ *Mark Twain*

—— DICE ——

The best throw of the dice is to throw them away.

——— DIET ———

Blessed are those who hunger and thirst, for they are sticking to their diets.   ~ *Troy Gordon*

There's a new diet that is supposed to really work. You only get to eat when there's good news.

When it comes to eating, you can sometimes help yourself more by helping yourself less.

~ *Richard Armour*

Eat a third, drink a third, and then leave the remaining third of your stomach empty. Then, if anger overtakes you, there will be room in it for gas.

~ *The Talmud*

——— DIFFICULTIES ———

Many men owe the grandeur of their lives to their tremendous difficulties.   ~ *Charles H. Spurgeon*

Difficulty is a severe instructor, set over us by the supreme ordinance of a parental guardian and legislator, who knows us better than we know ourselves; and he loves us better too. He that wrestles with us strengthens our nerves, and sharpens our skill. Our antagonist is our helper. This amicable conflict with difficulty obliges us to an intimate acquaintance with our object, and compels us to consider it in all its relations. It will not suffer us to be superficial.

~ *Edmund Burke*

...*ring*...

brethren, is the nurse of greatness—
...who roughly rocks her foster-children
...d athletic proportion.

DILIGENCE

One worthwhile task carried to a successful conclusion is worth half-a-hundred half-finished tasks.

~ *B.C. Forbes*

DISILLUSION

Disillusion is the child of illusion.

~ *Ron Lee Davis*

DIPLOMACY

Diplomacy is the art of saying "Nice doggie!" till you can find a rock.　　~ *Wynn Catlin*

To say nothing, especially when speaking, is half the art of diplomacy.　　~ *Will and Ariel Durant*

DIPLOMAT

A diplomat is a man who always remembers a woman's birthday but never remembers her age.

~ *Robert Frost*

A diplomat is a man who thinks twice before he says nothing.

——— DIRECTION ———

Any time the going seems easier, better check and see if you're not going downhill.

~ Megiddo Message

The world stands aside to let anyone pass who knows where he is going. *~ David Staff Jordan*

——— DISAGREEMENT ———

I disapprove of what you say, but I will defend to the death your right to say it. *~ Voltaire*

——— DISAPPOINTMENT ———

Blessed be he who expects nothing, for he shall never be disappointed. *~ Jonathan Swift*

——— DISCERNMENT ———

Any story sounds true until someone tells the other side and sets the record straight.

~ Proverbs 18:17

——— DISCIPLINE ———

If you refuse to discipline your son, it proves you don't love him; for if you love him you will be prompt to punish him.   ~*Proverbs 13:24*

Sometimes mere words are not enough—discipline is needed. For the words may not be heeded.

~*Proverbs 29:19*

He who will not answer to the rudder must answer to the rocks.

——— DISCONTENT ———

Restlessness and discontent are the first necessities of progress.   ~*Thomas Edison*

——— DISCOURAGEMENT ———

Never tell a young person that something cannot be done. God may have been waiting for countless centuries for somebody ignorant enough of the impossibility to do that thing.

I never allow myself to become discouraged under any circumstances.... The three great essentials to achieve anything worth while are, first, hard work; second, stick-to-it-iveness; third, common sense.

~ *Thomas Edison*

--------- **DISCRETION** ---------

A wise man restrains his anger and overlooks insults. This is to his credit. ~ *Proverbs 19:11*

Not every word requires an answer.

Never hold any one by the button or the hand in order to be heard out; for if people are unwilling to hear you, you had better hold your tongue than them.

~ *Lord Chesterfield*

--------- **DISOBEDIENCE** ---------

Disobedience is the worst of evils. This it is that ruins a nation. ~ *Jean Anouilh*

--------- **DOCTOR** ---------

The best doctors in the world are Dr. Diet, Dr. Quiet, and Dr. Merryman.

~ *Jonathan Swift*

Our doctor would never really operate unless it was necessary. He was just that way. If he didn't need the money, he wouldn't lay a hand on you.

~ *Herb Shriner*

The doctor is to be feared more than the disease.

~ *Latin Proverb*

Fate favors the physician by inventing lingering disease for which there is no cure, and the psychiatrists by inventing lingering cures for which there is no disease.

He has been a doctor a year now and has had two patients, no, three, I think—yes, it was three; I attended their funerals.   ~ *Mark Twain*

——— **DOUBT** ———

Don't doubt in the dark what God has revealed in the light.   ~ *V. Raymond Edman*

——— **DRINKING** ———

Wine gives false courage; hard liquor leads to brawls; what fools men are to let it master them, making them reel drunkenly down the street!

~ *Proverbs 20:1*

—— DRY ——

Some people are so dry that you might soak them in a joke for a month and it would not get through their skins.
~ Henry Ward Beecher

—— DUMB ——

While he was not dumber than an ox he was not any smarter.
~ James Thurber

—— ECONOMICS ——

You cannot strengthen the weak by weakening the strong. You cannot help the wage-earner by pulling down the wage-payer. You cannot help the poor by destroying the rich. You cannot help men permanently by doing for them what they could and should do for themselves.
~ Abraham Lincoln

If you're not confused you're not paying attention.
~ Wall Street Week

—— EDITOR ——

Editor: A person employed on a newspaper, whose business it is to separate the wheat from the chaff, and to see that the chaff is printed.
~ Elbert Hubbard

——— EDUCATION ———

Education is what's left over when you subtract what you've forgotten from what you've learned.

Sixty years ago I knew everything; now I know nothing; education is a progressive discovery of our own ignorance. ~ *Will Durant*

Perhaps the most valuable result of all education is the ability to make yourself do the thing you have to do, when it ought to be done, whether you like it or not.

~ *Thomas Huxley*

The chief end of higher education is not to make man dependent upon teachers but independent of them. ~ *L.D. Haskew*

Education is hanging around until you've caught on. ~ *Robert Frost*

The purpose of education is to provide everyone with the opportunity to learn how best he may serve the world.

If a man empties his purse into his head, no one can take it from him. ~ *Benjamin Franklin*

In the first place God made idiots. This was for practice. Then he made school boards.

~ *Mark Twain*

If nobody dropped out at the eighth grade, who would hire the college graduates?

There are lessons to be learned from a stupid man.

~ *Horace*

——— EFFORT ———

If you don't scale the mountain, you can't see the view.

Do a little more each day than you think you possibly can.   ~ *Lowell Thomas*

I have found it advisable not to give too much heed to what people say when I am trying to accomplish something of consequence. Invariably they proclaim it can't be done. I deem that the very best time to make the effort.   ~ *Calvin Coolidge*

——— EGGS ———

Put all your eggs in one basket, and—watch that basket.   ~ *Mark Twain*

——— EGOTIST ———

The last time I saw him he was walking down Lover's Lane holding his own hand.

~ *Fred Allen*

An egotist is not a man who thinks too much of himself. He is a man who thinks too little of other people. ~*J.F. Newton*

ELECT

The elect are the "whosoever wills"; the non-elect are the "whosoever won'ts." ~*D.L. Moody*

ELEPHANT

When you have got an elephant by the hind legs and he is trying to run away, it's best to let him run.

~*Abraham Lincoln*

ELOQUENCE

The finest eloquence is that which gets things done.

~*David Lloyd George*

EMPATHY

When we put ourselves in the other person's place, we're less likely to want to put him in his place.

~*Farmer's Digest*

If you wish to draw tears from me, you must first feel pain yourself.

——— ENCOURAGEMENT ———

Appreciation is thanking, recognition is seeing, and encouragement is bringing hope for the future.

Anxious hearts are very heavy but a word of encouragement does wonders!   *~ Proverbs 12:25*

Correction does much, but encouragement does more. Encouragement after censure is as the sun after a shower.   *~ Goethe*

——— ENDURANCE ———

And let us not get tired of doing what is right, for after a while we will reap a harvest of blessing if we don't get discouraged and give up.

~ Galatians 6:9

——— ENEMIES ———

Could we read the sacred history of our enemies, we should find in each man's life, sorrow and suffering enough to disarm all hostility.

*~ Henry Wadsworth
Longfellow*

If you have some enemies, you are to be congratulated, for no man ever amounted to much without arousing jealousies and creating enemies.

Your enemies are a very valuable asset as long as you refrain from striking back at them, because they keep you on the alert when you might become lazy.

Love your enemies, for they tell you your faults.
~ *Benjamin Franklin*

The Bible tells us to love our neighbors, and also to love our enemies; probably because they are generally the same people.   ~ *G.K. Chesterton*

Do not rejoice when your enemy meets trouble. Let there be no gladness when he falls—for the Lord may be displeased with you and stop punishing him!
~ *Proverbs 24:17, 18*

If your enemy is hungry, give him food! If he is thirsty, give him something to drink! This will make him feel ashamed of himself, and God will reward you.
~ *Proverbs 25:21, 22*

Man is his own worst enemy.
~ *Cicero*

Instead of loving your enemies, treat your friends a little better.   ~ *Ed Howe*

The best way to destroy your enemy is to make him your friend.   ~ *Abraham Lincoln*

——— ENGLAND ———

The British have a remarkable talent for keeping calm, even when there is no crisis.

~ Franklin P. Jones

——— ENJOYMENT ———

Enjoy what you can and endure what you must.

~ Goethe

——— ENTERPRISES ———

Beware of all enterprises that require new clothes.

~ Henry David Thoreau

——— ENTHUSIASM ———

Be intensely in earnest. Enthusiasm invites enthusiasm.
~ Russell H. Conwell

Every production of genius must be the production of enthusiasm.
~ Benjamin Disraeli

Nothing is so contagious as enthusiasm; it moves stones, it charms brutes. Enthusiasm is the genius of sincerity and thus accomplishes no victories without it.
~ Edward Bulwer-Lytton

ENVY

If there is any sin more deadly than envy, it is being pleased at being envied.   ~ *Richard Armour*

Envy takes the joy, happiness, and contentment out of living.   ~ *Billy Graham*

Love looks through a telescope; envy, through a microscope.

O, what a bitter thing it is to look into happiness through another man's eyes. ~ *William Shakespeare*

Man will do many things to get himself loved; he will do all things to get himself envied.

~ *Mark Twain*

To all my foes, dear fortune, send
Thy gifts! but never to my friend:
I tamely can endure the first;
But this with envy makes me burst.

~ *Jonathan Swift*

EPIGRAM

A brilliant epigram is a solemn platitude gone to a masquerade ball.   ~ *Lionel Strachey*

EQUALITY

We are all alike, on the inside.

~ *Mark Twain*

Inferiors revolt in order that they may be equal, and equals that they may be superior.

~ *Aristotle*

——— **ERROR** ———

An error is the more dangerous in proportion to the degree of truth which it contains.

~ *Henri Amiel*

Whatever is only almost true is quite false, and among the most dangerous of errors, because being so near truth, it is the more likely to lead astray.

~ *Henry Ward Beecher*

Error always rides the back of truth.

~ *R.E. Phillips*

There is no error so crooked, but it hath in it some lines of truth. ~ *M. Tupper*

——— **ETHICS** ———

I would rather be the man who bought the Brooklyn Bridge than the man who sold it.

~ *Will Rogers*

——— EVANGELISM ———

Evangelism is just one beggar telling another beggar where to find bread.   ~*D.T. Niles*

——— EVENTS ———

When I can't handle events, I let them handle themselves.   ~*Henry Ford*

Events of great consequence often spring from trifling circumstances.   ~*Livy*

——— EVIDENCE ———

Some circumstantial evidence is very strong, as when you find a trout in the milk.

~*Henry David Thoreau*

——— EVIL ———

Repay evil with good and you deprive the evildoer of all the pleasure of his wickedness.

~*Leo Tolstoy*

There is an evil which most of us condone and are even guilty of: indifference to evil. We remain neutral, impartial, and not easily moved by the wrongs done unto other people. Indifference to evil is more insidious than evil itself; it is more universal, more contagious, more dangerous.   ~*Abraham Jeschel*

Of two evils, choose neither.

~*Charles H. Spurgeon*

It is a sin to believe evil of others, but it is seldom a mistake.   ~*H.L. Mencken*

The love of evil is the root of all money.

~*American Proverb*

Most of the evils of life arise from man's being unable to sit still in a room. ~*Blaise Pascal*

——— EVOLUTION ———

The evolutionists seem to know everything about the missing link except the fact that it is missing.

~*G.K. Chesterton*

There is no more reason to believe that man descended from some inferior animal than there is to believe that a stately mansion has descended from a small cottage.   ~*W.J. Bryan*

Once I was a tadpole when I began to begin.
Then I was a frog with my tail tucked in.
Next I was a monkey on a coconut tree.
Now I am a doctor with a Ph.D.

EXAGGERATION

There are people so addicted to exaggeration that they can't tell the truth without lying.

~ Josh Billings

EXAMPLE

Example is not the main thing in influencing others. It is the only thing. *~ Albert Schweitzer*

Few things are harder to put up with than the annoyance of a good example.

~ Mark Twain

The first great gift we can bestow on others is a good example. *~ Thomas Morell*

EXCELLENCE

The pursuit of excellence is gratifying and healthy. The pursuit of perfection is frustrating, neurotic, and a terrible waste of time. *~ Edwin Bliss*

The secret of joy is contained in one word—excellence. To know how to do something well is to enjoy it.

~ *Pearl Buck*

——— EXCEPTIONS ———

The young man knows the rules, but the old man knows the exceptions.　　~ *Oliver W. Holmes*

——— EXERCISE ———

The only exercise some people get is jumping to conclusions, running down their friends, sidestepping responsibility, dodging issues, passing the buck, and pushing their luck.

I get my exercise acting as a pallbearer to my friends who exercise.　　~ *Chauncey Depew*

Whenever I feel like exercise, I lie down until the feeling passes.　　~ *Maynard Robert Hutchins*

The person who does not find time for exercise may have to find time for illness.

——— EXPECTATIONS ———

The more reasonable we are in our expectations, the fewer disappointments we will have in life.

~ *A. Nielen*

Blessed is he who expects nothing for he shall never be disappointed.   ~ *Jonathan Swift*

—— EXPENSES ——

If your outgo exceeds your income, your upkeep will be your downfall.   ~ *John M. Poure*

The cost of living is going up and the chance of living is going down.   ~ *Flip Wilson*

—— EXPERIENCE ——

The best substitute for experience is being sixteen.

~ *Raymond Duncan*

Truth divorced from experience will always dwell in the realms of doubt.   ~ *Henry Krause*

Experience is what you get when you were expecting something else.

Experience is the thing that enables you to recognize a mistake when you make it again.

~ *Bits and Pieces*

Experience is the worst teacher; it gives the test before explaining the lesson.

~ *Laurence Peter*

It's a wise man who profits by his own experience, but it's a good deal wiser one who lets the rattlesnake bite the other fellow.   *~ Josh Billings*

EXPERT

An expert is one who knows more and more about less and less.   *~ Nicholas Murray Butler*

EXPRESSION

Silence will not betray your thoughts but the expression on your face will.

EXTRAVAGANCE

The passion of acquiring riches in order to support a vain expense corrupts the purest souls.

~ Francois Fenelon

EYES

When a woman is speaking to you, listen to what she says with her eyes.   *~ Victor Hugo*

—— FACTS ——

Get your facts first, and then you can distort them as much as you please.   ~ *Mark Twain*

Facts are stubborn things.

~ *Smollett*

—— FAILURE ——

There are a lot of ways to become a failure, but never taking a chance is the most successful.

One of the reasons why mature people stop growing and learning is that they become less and less willing to risk failure.   ~ *John Gardner*

Ninety percent of all failures result from people quitting too soon.

I don't know the key to success, but the key to failure is trying to please everybody.

~ *Bill Cosby*

You can tell a failure by the way he criticizes success.

~ *Mel Johnson*

More men fail through lack of purpose than lack of talent.   ~ *Billy Sunday*

No man is a failure until he begins to blame somebody else. ~ *Bits and Pieces*

Failure is instructive. The person who really thinks learns quite as much from his failures as from his successes. ~ *John Dewey*

We mount to heaven mostly on the ruins of our cherished schemes, finding our failures were successes. ~ *Amos Bronson Alcott*

Who has never tasted what is bitter does not know what is sweet. ~ *German Proverb*

Failure is, in a sense, the highway to success, inasmuch as every discovery of what is false leads us to seek earnestly after what is true, and every fresh experience points out some form of error which we shall afterward carefully avoid.

—— FAIRNESS ——

Years have taught me at least one thing and that is not to try to avoid an unpleasant fact, but rather to grasp it firmly and let the other person observe I am at least treating him fairly. Then he, it has been my observation, will treat me in the same spirit.

~ *Benjamin Franklin*

How seldom we weigh our neighbor in the same balance with ourselves. ~ *Thomas à Kempis*

—— FAITH ——

If we desire an increase of faith, we must consent to its testings.

We live by faith or we do not live at all. Either we venture—or we vegetate. If we venture, we do so by faith simply because we cannot know the end of anything at its beginning. We risk marriage on faith or we stay single. We prepare for a profession by faith or we give up before we start. By faith we move mountains of opposition or we are stopped by molehills.

~ Harold Walker

Faith is like a toothbrush. Every man should have one and use it regularly, but he shouldn't try to use someone else's. *~ J.G. Stipe*

—— FAITHFULNESS ——

Nothing in life can take the place of faithfulness and dependability. It is one of the greatest virtues. Brilliance, genius, competence—all are subservient to the quality of faithfulness. *~ Walace Fridy*

A faithful employee is as refreshing as a cool day in the hot summertime. *~ Proverbs 25:13*

By working faithfully eight hours a day, you may eventually get to be a boss and work twelve hours a day.

~ Robert Frost

FALSEHOOD

Falsehoods not only disagree with truths, but usually quarrel among themselves.

~ *Daniel Webster*

FAME

Fame is proof that the people are gullible.

~ *Ralph Waldo Emerson*

I would rather that men ask ... why I have no statue than why I have one. ~ *Cato the Elder*

FAMILIARITY

Familiarity breeds contempt.

~ *Publilius Syrus*

Familiarity breeds contempt—and children.

~ *Mark Twain*

FAMILY

Happy families are all alike; every unhappy family is unhappy in its own way. ~ *Leo Tolstoy*

Every family tree has to have some sap.

There are nuts in every family tree.

A modern home is where the TV set is better adjusted than the kids.

See how a man treats his family, and you will see what his true feelings are about mankind.

The family you come from isn't as important as the family you're going to have. ~ *Ring Larder*

No family should attempt an auto trip if the kids outnumber the car windows.
~ *Terresa Bloomingdale*

God gives us relatives; thank God we can choose our friends. ~ *Ethel W. Mumford*

All people are your relatives, therefore expect only trouble from them. ~ *Chinese Proverb*

A happy family is but an earlier heaven.
~ *John Bowring*

——— **FASHION** ———

I see that fashion wears out more apparel than the man. ~ *William Shakespeare*

Fashion is a form of ugliness so intolerable that we have to alter it every six months.

~ *Oscar Wilde*

FAT

The minutes spent at the dinner table won't make you fat, but the seconds will.

FATHER

It is a wonderful heritage to have an honest father.
~ *Proverbs 20:7*

One father is more than a hundred schoolmasters.
~ *George Herbert*

He can climb the highest mountain or swim the biggest ocean. He can fly the fastest plane and fight the strongest tiger. But most of the time he just carries out the garbage.   ~ *Supervision*

FATIGUE

Fatigue makes cowards of us all.
~ *Vince Lombardi*

——— FAULTS ———

Best men are often moulded out of faults.

~ *William Shakespeare*

Every man should have a fair-sized cemetery in which to bury the faults of his friends.

~ *Henry Ward Beecher*

The greatest of all faults is to be conscious of none.

~ *Thomas Carlyle*

Faults are thick where love is thin.

~ *James Howell*

If we had no faults of our own, we should take less pleasure in noticing the faults of others.

~ *Francois
de La Rochefoucauld*

——— FEAR ———

To live with fear and not be afraid is the final test of maturity. ~ *Edward Weeks*

Nothing in life is to be feared. It is only to be understood. ~ *Marie Curie*

The only thing we have to fear is fear itself.

~ *Franklin Roosevelt*

Fear is the tax that conscience pays to guilt.

~ Swell

Keep your fears to yourself; share your courage with others. *~Robert Louis Stevenson*

One ought never to turn one's back on a threatened danger and try to run away from it. If you do that, you will double the danger. But if you meet it promptly and without flinching, you will reduce the danger by half. Never run away from anything. Never!

~ Winston Churchill

In the last resort nothing is ridiculous except the fear of being so. *~Henri Fauconnier*

You can conquer almost any fear if you will only make up your mind to do so. For remember, fear doesn't exist anywhere except in the mind.

~Dale Carnegie

Do the thing you fear, and the death of fear is certain. *~Ralph Waldo Emerson*

He who fears he will suffer, already suffers because of his fear. *~Michel de Montaigne*

Faint heart never won fair lady.

Our fears are always more numerous than our dangers.
~ *Seneca*

Present fears are less than horrible imaginings.
~ *William Shakespeare*

——— **FEELINGS** ———

The man who is always having his feelings hurt is about as pleasing a companion as a pebble in a shoe.
~ *Elbert Hubbard*

Never apologize for showing feelings. Remember that when you do, you apologize for the truth.
~ *Benjamin Disraeli*

The hardest thing to disguise is your feelings when you put a lot of relatives on the train for home.
~ *McKinney Frank Hubbard*

——— **FELLOWSHIP** ———

Searching for oneself within is as futile as peeling an onion to find the core: when you finish, there is nothing there but peelings; paradoxically, the only way to find oneself is to go outward to a genuine meeting with another.
~ *Sydney Harris*

FIDDLE

Perhaps it was because Nero played the fiddle, they burned Rome. *~Oliver Herford*

FISHING

There is no use in walking five miles to fish when you can depend on being as unsuccessful near home.

God does not deduct from man's allotted time those hours spent in fishing.

FLATTERY

Flattery is a trap; evil men are caught in it, but good men stay away and sing for joy.

~Proverbs 29:5, 6

When flatterers meet, the devil goes to dinner.

~Daniel Defoe

Nothing is so great an instance of ill manners as flattery. If you flatter all the company, you please none; if you flatter only one or two, you affront all the rest. *~Jonathan Swift*

He that flatters you more than you desire either has deceived you or wishes to deceive.

~Italian Proverb

Imitation is the sincerest [form] of flattery.

~ *Charles Colton*

——— FLIRTING ———

Flirting is wishful winking.

——— FOCUS ———

What we steadily, consciously, habitually think we are, that we tend to become.

~ *John Cowper Powers*

I recommend you take care of the minutes, for the hours will take care of themselves.

~ *Lord Chesterfield*

——— FOLLIES ———

The latter part of a wise man's life is taken up in curing the follies, prejudices, and false opinions he had contracted in the former.

~ *Jonathan Swift*

——— FOLLOW THROUGH ———

Consider the postage stamp: Its usefulness consists

in the ability to stick to one thing till it gets there.

~ *Josh Billings*

——— **FOOD** ———

I am allergic to food. Every time I eat, it breaks out in fat. ~*Jennifer Greene Duncan*

The most dangerous food a man can eat is wedding cake. ~ *American Proverb*

——— **FOOL** ———

A fool thinks he needs no advice, but a wise man listens to others. ~ *Proverbs 12:15*

Expectation is the fool's income.

Let us be thankful for the fools. But for them the rest of us could not succeed.

~ *Mark Twain*

Take all the fools out of this world and there wouldn't be any fun living in it, or profit.

~ *Josh Billings*

Fools rush in where fools have been before.

The best way to convince a fool that he is wrong is to let him have his own way. ~ *Josh Billings*

A man never knows what a fool he is until he hears himself imitated by one.   ~ *Herbert Tree*

April 1 is the day upon which we are reminded of what we are on the other three hundred sixty-four.

~ *Mark Twain*

Lord, what fools these mortals be!

~ *William Shakespeare*

——— FORCE ———

Justice without force is powerless; force without justice is tyrannical.   ~ *Blaise Pascal*

A man convinced against his will
Is of the same opinion still.

~ *Samuel Butler*

——— FOREIGN AID ———

Too often foreign aid is when the poor people of a rich nation send their money to the rich people of a poor nation.   ~ *Bits and Pieces*

——— FORGETFULNESS ———

There are three things I always forget. Names, faces—the third I can't remember.

~ *Italo Svevo*

─── FORGETTING ───

I've a grand memory for forgetting.

~ *Robert Louis Stevenson*

─── FORGIVENESS ───

God, you forgive them...because if we both do then they will get off scot free.

If you are suffering from a bad man's injustice, forgive him lest there be two bad men.

~ *Augustine*

Always forgive your enemies—nothing annoys them so much. ~ *Oscar Wilde*

He that cannot forgive others breaks the bridge over which he must pass himself; for every man has need to be forgiven. ~ *Thomas Fuller*

To be wronged is nothing unless you continue to remember it. ~ *Confucius*

Forgive your enemies, but never forget their names.

~ *John F. Kennedy*

Forgiveness is the fragrance the violet sheds on the heel that has crushed it. ~ *Mark Twain*

There's no point in burying a hatchet if you're going to put up a marker on the site.

~ *Sydney Harris*

A good memory is fine—but the ability to forget is the true test of greatness.

It is easier to forgive an enemy than a friend.

~ *Dorothee Deluzy*

Forgiveness is surrendering my right to hurt you back if you hurt me.   ~ *Archibald Hart*

Forgiveness is not a feeling but a promise or commitment to three things: 1) I will not use it against them in the future, 2) I will not talk to others about them, 3) I will not dwell on it myself.

~ *Jay E. Adams*

The grease of forgiving love can reduce the friction and salve the irritation. Forgiveness is not holy amnesia which erases the past—instead it is the experience of healing that draws the poison out. You may recall that hurt but you will not relive the hurt. The hornet of memory may fly again, but forgiveness has drawn out the sting.   ~ *David Augsburger*

Without forgiveness life is governed by an endless cycle of resentment and retaliation.

~ *Roberto Assagioli*

Only the brave know how to forgive.

To understand is to forgive.

There is no revenge so complete as forgiveness.

~ *Josh Billings*

He who has not forgiven an enemy has never yet tasted one of the most sublime enjoyments of life.

~ *Johann Lavater*

A Christian will find it cheaper to pardon than to resent. Forgiveness saves the expense of anger, the cost of hatred, the waste of spirits.

~ *Hannah More*

—— **FORTUNE** ——

Fortune favors the bold but abandons the timid.

—— **FRANKNESS** ——

It is an honor to receive a frank reply.

~ *Proverbs 24:26*

—— **FREEDOM** ——

Freedom is like a coin. It has the word privilege on one side and responsibility on the other. It does not have privilege on both sides. There are too many today who want everything involved in privilege but refuse to accept anything that approaches the sense of responsibility. ~ *Joseph Sizoo*

Freedom is opportunity to make decisions. Character is ability to make right decisions. It can be achieved only in a climate of freedom. For no one learns to make right decisions without being free to make wrong ones.

~ *Kenneth Sollitt*

—— FRIEND ——

Nothing is there more friendly to a man than a friend in need. ~ *Plautus*

The Holy Passion of Friendship is of so sweet and steady and loyal and enduring a nature that it will last through a whole lifetime, if not asked to lend money.

~ *Mark Twain*

Before borrowing money from a friend, decide which you need most. ~ *American Proverb*

Never speak ill of yourself. Your friends will always say enough on that subject. ~ *Charles Talleyrand*

Friendship may, and often does, grow into love; but love never subsides into friendship.

~ *Lord Byron*

If all persons knew what they said of each other, there would not be four friends in the world.

~ Blaise Pascal

Your friend is the man who knows all about you, and still likes you.   *~ Elbert Hubbard*

Real friends are those who, when you've made a fool of yourself, don't feel that you've done a permanent job.

I desire so to conduct the affairs of this administration that if at the end, when I come to lay down the reins of power, I have lost every other friend on earth, I shall at least have one friend left, and that friend shall be down inside of me.   *~ Abraham Lincoln*

A friend is a person with whom you dare to be yourself.

He is my friend because we have so many faults in common.

Go often to the house of your friend, for weeds soon choke up the unused path.   *~ William Shakespeare*

Friends are made by many acts—and lost by only one.

A friend is one who comes to you when all others leave.

Good company in a journey makes the way seem the shorter.   ~ *Izaak Walton*

A friend is one who has the same enemies you have.
                    ~ *Abraham Lincoln*

A mirror reflects a man's face, but what he is really like is shown by the kind of friends he chooses.
                    ~ *Proverbs 27:19*

There are not many things in life so beautiful as true friendship, and there are not many things more uncommon.   ~ *Megiddo Message*

One should keep his friendships in constant repair.
                    ~ *Samuel Johnson*

A real friend is a person who, when you've made a fool of yourself, lets you forget it.
                    ~ *Bits and Pieces*

Friendship is like Rome. It's not built in a day.
                    ~ *Franklin P. Jones*

You can make more friends in two months by becoming interested in other people than you can in two years by trying to get other people interested in you.   ~ *Dale Carnegie*

My best friend is the one who brings out the best in me.   ~ *Henry Ford*

A friend is a person who does his knocking before he enters instead of after he leaves.

~ *Irene Keepin*

A valuable friend is one who'll tell you what you should be told, even if it offends you.

~ *Frank A. Clark*

Friendship will not stand the strain of very much good advice for very long.   ~ *Robert Lynd*

Three men are my friends. He that loves me, he that hates me, he that is indifferent to me. Who loves me teaches me tenderness. Who hates me teaches me caution. Who is indifferent to me teaches me self-reliance.

~ *Parin*

If you want enemies, excel your friends; but if you want friends, let your friends excel you.

~ *Francois
de La Rochefoucauld*

He who seeks friends without faults stays forever without friends.

Friends are people who stick together until debt do them part.

A friend is a person who goes around saying nice things about you behind your back.

Prosperity begets friends; adversity proves them.

A friend is one before whom I may think aloud.
> ~ *Ralph Waldo Emerson*

It's smart to pick your friends—but not to pieces.

God save me from my friends, I can protect myself from my enemies.   ~ *Marshal de Villars*

Friends are like melons. Shall I tell you why? To find one good, you must a hundred try.
> ~ *Claude Mermet*

A true friend is one soul in two bodies.
> ~ *Aristotle*

The only way to have a friend is to be one.
> ~ *Ralph Waldo Emerson*

Animals are such agreeable friends—they ask no questions, they pass no criticisms.
> ~ *George Eliot*

A friend must not be injured, even in jest.
> ~ *Publilius Syrus*

True friendship is a plant of slow growth and must undergo and withstand the shocks of adversity before it is entitled to the appellation.
> ~ *Washington*

Friendship, of itself a holy tie,
Is made more sacred by adversity.

~ *John Dryden*

Friendship improves happiness, and abates misery, by doubling our joy, and dividing our grief.

~ *Joseph Addison*

To let friendship die away by negligence and silence is certainly not wise. It is voluntarily to throw away one of the greatest comforts of this weary pilgrimage.

~ *Samuel Johnson*

Every house where love abides and friendship is a guest, is surely home, and home, sweet home; for there the heart can rest.   ~ *Henry Van Dyke*

Friendships last when each friend thinks he has a slight superiority over the other.

~ *Honore de Balzac*

Friendship is to be purchased only by friendship.

The light of friendship is like the light of phosphorus, seen when all around is dark.

He who wants a long friendship should develop a short memory.

——— FRUSTRATION ———

Frustration is the emotional battle we face when tasks or goals are not accomplished.

FUNNY

Everything is funny as long as it is happening to somebody else.   ~ *Will Rogers*

FUNNYBONE

One of the best things a man can have up his sleeve is a funnybone.

FURY

The full potentialities of human fury cannot be reached until a friend of both parties tactfully intervenes.   ~ *G.K. Chesterton*

FUTURE

The best thing about the future is that it comes only one day at a time.   ~ *Abraham Lincoln*

My interest is in the future because I am going to spend the rest of my life there.

~ *Charles F. Kettering*

GAMBLE

He who gambles picks his own pocket.

The only man that makes money following the races is the one who does so with a broom and shovel.

~ Elbert Hubbard

GAS

We're overlooking one of the biggest sources of natural gas in the country—politicians.

~ Herb True

GENERATION

I was born in the wrong generation. When I was a young man, no one had any respect for youth. Now I am an old man and no one has any respect for age.

~ Bertrand Russell

GENEROUS

We're all generous, but with different things, like time, money, talent—criticism.

~ Frank A. Clark

GENIUS

Everyone is born a genius, but the process of living degeniuses them.   *~ Buckminster Fuller*

——— GENTLEMAN ———

To be born a gentleman is an accident—to die one is an accomplishment.

A gentleman is a gentleman the world over; loafers differ. ~ *George Bernard Shaw*

——— GENTLENESS ———

Nothing is so strong as gentleness; nothing so gentle as real strength. ~ *St. Francis de Sales*

Gentleness springs from great strength.

~ *R.E. Phillips*

——— GIFT ———

He that parts with his property before his death prepares himself for much suffering.

~ *French Proverb*

——— GIVING ———

It's better to give than to lend, and it costs about the same. ~ *Philip Gibbs*

There is no grace in a benefit that sticks to the fingers.   ~ *Seneca*

If you are not generous with a meager income, you will never be generous with abundance.

~ *Harold Nye*

When it comes to giving, some people stop at nothing.

Money-giving is a good criterion of a person's mental health. Generous people are rarely mentally ill people.   ~ *Dr. Karl Menninger*

Some say, "I've given him the shirt off my back and now look what he has done to me," or "I've given him the best years of my life and look at what I get in return." If we bestow a gift or a favor and expect a return for it, it is no gift but a trade.

~ *Good Reading*

No person was ever honored for what he received. Honor has been the reward for what he gave.

~ *Calvin Coolidge*

Those who give hoping to be rewarded with honor are not giving, they are bargaining.

~ *Philo*

You only keep what you give away.

~ *R.E. Phillips*

It is one of the most beautiful compensations of this life that no man can sincerely try to help another without helping himself. ~*Ralph Waldo Emerson*

Do your giving while you're living, so you're knowing where it's going. ~*Donald Sumner French*

What you keep to yourself, you lose; what you give away, you keep forever.

——— GLANCE ———

He who looketh upon a woman loseth a fender.

——— GOAT ———

If someone is always trying to get your goat, maybe it's because your goat is a nuisance to everyone.

——— GOD ———

What a vast distance there is between knowing God and loving him! ~*Blaise Pascal*

A pastor visited a family whose son had been killed in an automobile accident. He heard the mother rail out at him: "Where was your God when my boy was killed?" He quietly said, "The same place he was when his Son was killed." ~*Roger Lovette*

You have laughed God out of your schools, out of your books, and out of your life, but you cannot laugh him out of your death. ~ *Dagobert Runes*

——— GOLF ———

Golf is like a love affair: If you don't take it seriously, it's no fun; if you do take it seriously, it breaks your heart. ~ *Arnold Daly*

——— GOOD DEEDS ———

The greatest pleasure I know is to do a good action by stealth and have it found out by accident.

~ *Charles Lamb*

——— GOOD HUMOR ———

Good humor makes all things tolerable.

~ *Henry Ward Beecher*

——— GOOD NEWS ———

Good news from far away is like cold water to the thirsty. ~ *Proverbs 25:25*

——— GOSSIP ———

An evil man sows strife; gossip separates the best of friends.   *~Proverbs 16:28*

Don't tell your secrets to a gossip unless you want them broadcast to the world.

~Proverbs 20:19

Fire goes out for lack of fuel, and tensions disappear when gossip stops.   *~Proverbs 26:20*

Gossip is a dainty morsel eaten with great relish.

~Proverbs 26:22

I am more deadly than the screaming shell from the howitzer. I win without killing. I tear down homes, break hearts, and wreck lives. I travel on the wings of the wind. No innocence is strong enough to intimidate me, no purity pure enough to daunt me. I have no regard for truth, no respect for justice, no mercy for the defenseless. My victims are as numerous as the sands of the sea, and often as innocent. I never forget and seldom forgive. My name is Gossip.

~Morgan Blake

Gossip is when you hear something you like about someone you don't.   *~Earl Wilson*

A gossip is a person who will never tell a lie if the truth will do as much damage.

He who relates the faults of others to you will relate your faults to the other fellow.

~ *Grit*

Not everyone repeats gossip. Some improve it.

~ *Franklin P. Jones*

Conversation between Adam and Eve must have been difficult at times because they had nobody to talk about.

~ *Agnes Repplier*

If we all said to each other's faces what we say behind each other's backs, society would be impossible.

~ *Honore de Balzac*

It is easier for a woman to defend her virtue against men than her reputation against women.

~ *French Proverb*

Hear no evil, see no evil, speak no evil—and you'll never be invited to a party.

He who gossips lets the chat out of the bag.

Don't talk about yourself; it will be done when you leave.

~ *Addison Mizner*

—— GOVERNMENT ——

It's a good thing we don't get all the government we pay for.

Nothing is easier than the expenditure of public money. It doesn't appear to belong to anyone. The temptation is overwhelming to bestow it on somebody.

~ Calvin Coolidge

No man undertakes a trade he has not learned, even the meanest; yet everyone thinks himself sufficiently qualified for the hardest of all trades, that of government.   *~ Socrates*

There's no trick to being a humorist when you have the whole government working for you.

~ Will Rogers

——— GRATEFULNESS ———

He who is carried on another's back does not appreciate how far the town is.   *~ African Proverb*

——— GRATITUDE ———

Next to ingratitude, the most painful thing to bear is gratitude.   *~ Henry Ward Beecher*

He who receives a benefit with gratitude repays the first installment on his debt.

——— GREATNESS ———

Greatness lies not in being strong, but in the right use of strength. ~ *Henry Ward Beecher*

I studied the lives of great men and famous women, and I found that the men and women who got to the top were those who did the jobs they had in hand, with everything they had of energy and enthusiasm and hard work. ~ *Harry S. Truman*

The greatest truths are the simplest—and so are the greatest men. ~ *Augustus Hare*

Speaking generally, no man appears great to his contemporaries, for the same reason that no man is great to his servants—both know too much of him.

~ *Charles Colton*

There is a great person who makes every person feel small. But the real great person is the person who makes every person feel great.

~ *G.K. Chesterton*

He who comes up to his own idea of greatness must always have had a very low standard of it in his mind.

~ *William Hazlitt*

——— **GREED** ———

One thing you can say for greed: It's responsible for some imaginative rationalizations.

The weakness of this age is our inability to distinguish our needs from our greeds.

——— **GRIEF** ———

Every substantial grief has twenty shadows, and most of them shadows of your own making.

Grief knits two hearts in closer bonds than happiness ever can; and common sufferings are far stronger links than common joys.   ~*Alphonse de Lamartine*

Where grief is fresh, any attempt to divert it only irritates.   ~*Samuel Johnson*

Everyone can master a grief but he that has it.

~*William Shakespeare*

——— **GROUCH** ———

Grouches are nearly always pinheads, small men who have never made any effort to improve their mental capacity.   ~*Thomas Edison*

——— GROWL ———

Growl all day and you'll feel dog tired at night.

——— GROWTH ———

People, like trees, must grow or die. There's no standing still. A tree dies when its roots become blocked. A human being becomes mentally and spiritually, and eventually physically, dead when the circumstances of his life keep him from achieving. Psychologists and sociologists spend their lives trying to patch up individuals and institutions that have stopped growing.   *~Joseph Shore*

——— GUESTS ———

After three days, fish and guests stink.
                              ~John Lyly

Unbidden guests are often welcomest when they are gone.   *~William Shakespeare*

——— GUILT ———

A guilty conscience is the mother of invention.
                              ~Carolyn Wells

——— HABIT ———

Reason stands small show against the entrenched power of habit.   ~ *Elbert Hubbard*

The mind unlearns with difficulty what it has long learned.   ~ *Seneca*

Habit, if not resisted, soon becomes necessity.

~ *Augustine*

Habits are at first cobwebs, then cables.

~ *Spanish Proverb*

The unfortunate thing about this world is that good habits are so much easier to give up than bad ones.

~ *Somerset Maugham*

The best way to break a bad habit is to drop it.

~ *D.S. Yoder*

The chains of habit are too weak to be felt until they are too strong to be broken.

——— HALF-WIT ———

The real wit tells jokes to make others feel superior, while the half-wit tells them to make others feel small.

~ *Elmer Wheeler*

——— HAPPINESS ———

Happiness is not an end product in itself. It is a by-product of working, playing, loving, and living.

~ Haim Ginott

Happiness? That's nothing more than health and a poor memory. *~ Albert Schweitzer*

What a wonderful life I've had! I only wish I'd realized it sooner. *~ Colette*

Happiness is not a state to arrive at, but a manner of traveling. *~ Margaret Lee Runbeck*

Happiness is the natural flower of duty.

~ Phillips Brooks

To be happy, add not to your possessions but subtract from your desires. *~ Seneca*

People will be happy in about the same degree that they are helpful.

Happiness is a perfume which you can't pour on someone without getting some on yourself.

~ Ralph Waldo Emerson

There is only one way to happiness and that is to cease worrying about things which are beyond the power of our will. *~ Epictetus*

Happiness is possible only when one is busy.

I have noticed that folks are generally about as happy as they have made up their minds to be.

We are never so happy, nor so unhappy, as we suppose ourselves to be. ~ *Francois*
de La Rochefoucauld

———— **HAPPY-GO-LUCKY** ————

Being happy-go-lucky around a person whose heart is heavy is as bad as stealing his jacket in cold weather, or rubbing salt in his wounds.

~ *Proverbs 25:20*

———— **HARVEST** ————

Whatsoever a man soweth, that shall he also reap.

~ *Galatians 6:7 (TLB)*

———— **HASTE** ————

Make haste slowly.

Hasty climbers have sudden falls.

~ *Italian Proverb*

Haste makes waste.   ~ *English Proverb*

—— **HATCHET** ——

Nobody ever forgets where he buried a hatchet.

~ *McKinney Frank
Hubbard*

—— **HATE** ——

It is better to eat soup with someone you love than steak with someone you hate.

~ *Proverbs 15:17*

Great hate follows great love.

~ *Irish Proverb*

Hating people is like burning down your own home to get rid of a rat.   ~ *Harry Emerson Fosdick*

Some persons, by hating vice too much, come to love men too little.

Don't introduce me to that man! I want to go on hating him, and I can't hate a man whom I know.

~ *Charles Lamb*

Hatred is self-punishment.

A man with hate in his heart may sound pleasant enough, but don't believe him; for he is cursing you in his heart. Though he pretends to be so kind, his hatred will finally come to light for all to see.

~ *Proverbs 26:24-26*

Hatred is the coward's revenge for being intimidated. ~ *George Bernard Shaw*

——— HEADS OR TAILS ———

The Lord gave you two ends, one for sitting and one for thinking. Your success depends upon which you use. Heads you win; tails you lose.

——— HEALTH ———

The poorest man would not part with health for money, but the richest would gladly part with all his money for health. ~ *Charles Colton*

——— HEARING ———

It is a foolish man that hears all he hears.

~ *Austin O'Malley*

—— HEART ——

A happy face means a glad heart; a sad face means a breaking heart. *~Proverbs 15:13*

A merry heart maketh a cheerful countenance.
~Proverbs 15:13 (KJV)

Where your treasure is, there will your heart be also. *~Matthew 6:21 (KJV)*

Keep your heart right, even when it is sorely wounded. *~J.C. Macaulay*

—— HEAVEN ——

Heaven goes by favour. If it went by merit, you would stay out and your dog would go in.

~Mark Twain

—— HELL ——

I never give them hell. I just tell the truth and they think it's hell. *~Harry S. Truman*

It does not require a decision to go to hell.

The safest road to hell is the gradual one—the gentle slope, soft underfoot, without sudden turnings, without milestones, without signposts.

~C.S. Lewis

Hell begins on the day when God grants us a clear vision of all that we might have achieved, of all the gifts which we have wasted, or all that we might have done which we did not do.... For me the conception of hell lies in two words: Too Late.

~ *Gian-Carlo Menotti*

Hell is paved with good intentions.

~ *St. Bernard*

——— HELP ———

Sometimes nothing gives you a helping hand like receiving a kick in the pants.

If you ever need a helping hand, you'll find one at the end of your arm.   ~ *Yiddish Proverb*

——— HERO ———

Show me a hero and I will write you a tragedy.

~ *F. Scott Fitzgerald*

We can't all be heroes because someone has to sit on the curb and clap as they go by.

~ *Will Rogers*

I've had several years in Hollywood and I still think the movie heroes are in the audience.

~ *Wilson Mizner*

———— HISTORY ————

History maketh a young man to be old, without wrinkles or gray hairs, privileging him with the experience of age, without either the infirmities or inconveniences thereof.   ~ *Fuller*

Those who cannot remember the past are condemned to repeat it.   ~ *George Santayana*

Any event, once it has occurred, can be made to appear inevitable by some competent historian.

~ *Lee Simonson*

History is the discovering of the constant and universal principles of human nature.

~ *David Hume*

We Americans are the best informed people on earth as to the events of the last twenty-four hours; we are not the best informed as to the events of the last sixty centuries.   ~ *Will and Ariel Durant*

When you read history it is quite astonishing to discover that there never was a day when men thought times were really good. Every generation in history has been haunted by the feeling of crisis.

~ *Harold Walker*

Human history is in essence a history of ideas.

~*H.G. Wells*

—— HITLER ——

Hitler had the best answers to everything.

~*Charles Manson*

—— HOLLYWOOD ——

Hollywood: A place where people from Iowa mistake each other for movie stars.

~*Fred Allen*

Hollywood: A place where the inmates are in charge of the asylum.   ~*Laurence Stallings*

Strip away the phony tinsel of Hollywood and you will find the real tinsel underneath.

~*Oscar Levant*

—— HOLY SPIRIT ——

Though every believer has the Holy Spirit, the Holy Spirit does not have every believer.

~*A.W. Tozer*

─────── **HOME** ───────

The number of accidents in the home is rising; people aren't spending enough time there to know their way around.

The strength of a nation is derived from the integrity of its homes.   ~ *Confucius*

He is the happiest, be king or peasant, who finds peace in his home.   ~ *Goethe*

Home is a field where there may be grown character, nobility, and song, or where by neglect may grow the thorn tree of strife and the bramble bush of discontent.

Home is what you make it. Home is heaven or hell. It is a residence for angels or a dungeon filled with demons.   ~ *Oliver Wilson*

> I suppose I passed it a hundred times,
> But I always stop for a minute
> And look at the house, the tragic house,
> The house with nobody in it.
>
> ~ *Joyce Kilmer*

Mid pleasures and places though we may roam,
Be it ever so humble, there's no place like home.

~ *J. Howard Payne*

——— HONESTY ———

Even a little lie is dangerous; it deteriorates the conscience. And the importance of conscience is eternal, like love.   *~Pablo Casals*

There's one way to find out if a man is honest—ask him. If he says, "Yes," you know he is a crook.

~Groucho Marx

A man can build a staunch reputation for honesty by admitting he was in error, especially when he gets caught at it.   *~Robert Ruark*

Honesty pays, but it doesn't seem to pay enough to suit some people.   *~Kin Hubbard*

No matter how brilliant a man may be, he will never engender confidence in his subordinates and associates if he lacks simple honesty and moral courage.

~J. Lawton Collins

An honest man's the noblest work of God.

~Alexander Pope

I do not know what the heart of a rascal may be, but I know what is in the heart of an honest man; it is horrible.   *~Joseph de Maistre*

Honesty is the best policy.

~Cervantes

HONOR

HONEYMOON

Their honeymoon is over when he phones that he'll be late for supper—and she has already left a note that it's in the refrigerator.   *~ Bill Lawrence*

HONOR

If somebody throws a brick at me, I can catch it and throw it back. But when somebody awards a decoration to me, I am out of words.

~ Harry S. Truman

It is better to deserve honors and not have them than to have them and not deserve them.

~ Mark Twain

The louder he talked of his honor, the faster we counted our spoons.   *~ Ralph Waldo Emerson*

HOPE

There is no medicine like hope, no incentive so great, and no tonic so powerful as expectation of something better tomorrow. *~ Orison Marden*

Hope deferred makes the heart sick; but when dreams come true at last, there is life and joy.

~ Proverbs 13:12

Take from a man his wealth, and you hinder him; take from him his purpose, and you slow him down. But take from man his hope, and you stop him. He can go on without wealth, and even without purpose, for awhile. But he will not go on without hope.

~ *C. Neil Strait*

——— HORSES ———

You may lead a horse to water but you can't make him drink. ~ *English Proverb*

——— HOSPITAL ———

A hospital should also have a recovery room adjoining the cashier's office. ~ *Francis O'Walsh*

——— HOUSE ———

He that lives in a glass house must not throw stones.
~ *English Proverb*

A foolish man...built his house upon the sand.
~ *Matthew 7:26 (KJV)*

——— HUM-DRUM ———

After all, if you are living a hum-drum life, and you

do nothing to change it, ten years from now you will be a product of ten more years of hum-drumidness.

~ David Campbell

—— **HUMAN** ——

To err is human, but when the eraser wears out ahead of the pencil, you're overdoing it.

~ J. Jenkins

—— **HUMANITY** ——

Human action can be modified to some extent, but human nature cannot be changed.

~ Abraham Lincoln

—— **HUMBLE** ——

Be humble or you'll stumble.

~ D.L. Moody

—— **HUMILITY** ——

The more humble a man is before God, the more he will be exalted; the more humble he is before man, the more he will get rode roughshod.

~ Josh Billings

Humility is to make a right estimate of one's self.

~ *Charles H. Spurgeon*

—— HUMOR ——

A well-developed sense of humor is the pole that adds balance to your steps as you walk the tightrope of life.   ~ *William A. Ward*

If you could choose one characteristic that would get you through life, choose a sense of humor.

~ *Jennifer Jones*

There are many humorous things in the world, among them the white man's notion that he is less savage than other savages.   ~ *Mark Twain*

Fear not a jest. If one throws salt at thee thou wilt receive no harm unless thou hast sore places.

~ *Latin Proverb*

When humor is meant to be taken seriously, it's no joke.   ~ *Lionel Strachey*

I think the next best thing to solving a problem is finding some humor in it.   ~ *Frank A. Clark*

A person without a sense of humor is like a wagon without springs—jolted by every pebble in the road.

~ *Henry Ward Beecher*

Defining and analyzing humor is a pastime of humorless people. ~ *Robert Benchley*

There are very few good judges of humor, and they don't agree. ~ *Josh Billings*

HUNGER

It is a lot easier emotionally to handle the fact that millions of people are starving if we don't see them as individuals. ~ *Stan Mooneyham*

Hungry bellies have no ears.

~ *Francois Rabelais*

An empty stomach is not a good political adviser.

~ *Albert Einstein*

HURTS

Do we share our hurts or memorize them?

In this life we will encounter hurts and trials that we will not be able to change; we are just going to have to allow them to change us. ~ *Ron Lee Davis*

——— HUSBAND ———

An archaeologist is the best husband any woman can have: the older she gets, the more interested he is in her.   ~*Agatha Christie*

A good husband makes a good wife.

It's a sad house where the hen crows louder than the cock.   ~*Scottish Proverb*

Some husbands know all the answers; they've been listening for years.

As the husband is, the wife is.

~*Lord Tennyson*

——— HYPOCRISY ———

A hypocrite is like the man who murdered both his parents and then pleaded for mercy on the grounds that he was an orphan.   ~*Abraham Lincoln*

The wicked work harder to preach hell than the righteous do to get to heaven.

~*American Proverb*

——— IRS ———

April showers are the tears shed over taxes paid to the IRS.

—— IDEALISM ——

Idealism increases in direct proportion to one's distance from the problem.   *~John Galsworthy*

—— IDEAS ——

With no ideas of diamonds, we settle for glass.

Ideas are funny things. They don't work unless you do.

The ideas I stand for are not mine. I borrowed them from Socrates. I swiped them from Chesterfield. I stole them from Jesus. And I put them in a book. If you don't like their rules, whose would you use?

~ Dale Carnegie

There is one thing stronger than all the armies in the world and that is an idea whose time has come.

~ Victor Hugo

Sometimes a person's mind is stretched by a new idea and never does go back to its old dimensions.

~ O   *Wendell H*

Nothing is more dangerous th
the only one we have.   *~ J*

Almost all really new ideas h
foolishness when they are first

He can compress the most words into the smallest idea of any man I ever met. ~ *Abraham Lincoln*

A new idea is delicate. It can be killed by a sneer or a yawn; it can be stabbed to death by a quip and worried to death by a frown on the right man's brow.

~ *Charles Brower*

It's tough watching a good idea lose because its backers are less eloquent or have less clout than its opponents. ~ *Lester Case*

Ideas are like children—no matter how much you admire someone else's you can't help liking your own best.

——— IDLE ———

Idle folks have the least leisure.

By doing nothing we learn to do ill.

The man with time to burn never gave the world any light.

lle folks lack no excuses.

who have nothing to do are quickly tired of mpany. ~ *Collier*

It is a great weariness to do nothing.

Idle people are dead people that you can't bury.

A sluggard takes a hundred steps because he would not take one in due time.

An idle brain is the devil's workshop.

Prolonged idleness paralyzes initiative.

No one has a right to live in idleness and expect to live long and be happy. The ship anchored in the harbor rots faster than the ship crossing the ocean; a still pond of water stagnates more rapidly than a running stream. Our unused minds are subject to atrophy much more rapidly than those in use. The unused cells in our brains deteriorate much faster than those which are continually exercised. Hence, to remain young we must remain active. *~ American Salesman*

——— IGNORANCE ———

You can say one thing for ignorance—it certainly causes a lot of interesting arguments.

Ignorance is never out of style. It was in fashion yesterday, it is the rage today, and it will set the pace tomorrow. *~ Frank Dane*

Ignorance of the law must not prevent the losing lawyer from collecting his fee.

~ *Legal Maxim*

A jury is a group of twelve people of average ignorance. ~ *Herbert Spencer*

The older we grow the greater becomes our wonder at how much ignorance one can contain without bursting one's clothes. ~ *Mark Twain*

I have never met a man so ignorant that I couldn't learn something from him. ~ *Galileo Galilei*

When I was a boy of fourteen, my father was so ignorant I could hardly stand to have the old man around. But when I got to be twenty-one, I was astonished at how much the old man had learned.

~ *Mark Twain*

——— IGNORE ———

Parents were invented to make children happy by giving them something to ignore.

~ *Ogden Nash*

——— ILLUSTRATIONS ———

The sermon is the house; the illustrations are the windows that let in the light.

~ *Charles H. Spurgeon*

IMAGINATION

When you stop having dreams and ideals—well, you might as well stop altogether.

IMITATION

Imitation is the sincerest [form] of flattery.

~ *Charles Colton*

He who imitates what is evil always goes beyond the example that is set; on the contrary, he who imitates what is good always falls short.

~ *Francesco Guicciardini*

IMPOSSIBILITY

You can't get blood out of a turnip.

~ *English Proverb*

You can't make a silk purse out of a sow's ear.

~ *English Proverb*

IMPOSSIBLE

The difficult we do immediately, the impossible takes a little longer.

IMPROMPTU

It usually takes me more than three weeks to prepare a good impromptu speech.

~ *Mark Twain*

IMPROVEMENT

People seldom improve when they have no other model but themselves to copy after.

~ *Oliver Goldsmith*

INCOME

I'm living so far beyond my income that we may almost be said to be living apart.

~ *Hector Munro*

Live within your income, even if you have to borrow money to do so. ~ *Josh Billings*

INCOME TAX

Income-tax forms should be made more realistic by allowing the taxpayer to list Uncle Sam as a dependent.

INCOMPATIBILITY

A little incompatibility is the spice of life,

particularly if he has income and she is pattable.

~ *Ogden Nash*

—— INDECISION ——

Don't stand shivering upon the bank; plunge in at once, and have it over. ~ *Sam Slick*

—— INDEPENDENCE ——

When I was a boy I used to do what my father wanted. Now I have to do what my boy wants. My problem is: When am I going to do what I want?

~ *Sam Levenson*

—— INDIVIDUALITY ——

An institution is the lengthened shadow of one man. ~*Ralph Waldo Emerson*

—— INDULGENCE ——

Do you like honey? Don't eat too much of it, or it will make you sick! ~ *Proverbs 25:16*

—— INDUSTRY ——

Whatsoever thy hand findeth to do, do it with thy might. ~ *Ecclesiastes 9:10 (KJV)*

In the ordinary business of life, industry can do anything which genius can do, and very many things which it cannot.　　*~ Henry Ward Beecher*

The bread earned by the sweat of the brow is thrice blessed bread, and it is far sweeter than the tasteless loaf of idleness.　　*~ Crowquill*

—— **INFERIOR** ——

No one can make you feel inferior without your consent.　　*~ Eleanor Roosevelt*

—— **INFLATION** ——

Try to save money. Someday it may be valuable again.

—— **INFLUENCE** ——

Ten persons who speak make more noise than ten thousand who are silent.　　*~ Napoleon*

The best way for a young man who is without friends or influence to begin is: first, to get a position; second, to keep his mouth shut; third, observe; fourth, be faithful; fifth, make his employer think he would be lost in a fog without him; sixth, be polite.

~ Russell Sage

INGRATITUDE

He that has satisfied his thirst turns his back on the well.
~*Baltasar Gracian*

INHERITANCE

We pay for the mistakes of our ancestors, and it seems only fair that they should leave us the money to pay with.
~*Don Marquis*

INJUSTICE

He who commits injustice is ever made more wretched than he who suffers it.

~*Plato*

INNUENDO

Life would be a perpetual flea hunt if a man were obliged to run down all the innuendoes, inveracities, insinuations, and misrepresentations which are uttered against him.
~*Henry Ward Beecher*

INSANITY

Insanity is hereditary, you can get it from your children.
~*Sam Levenson*

Though this be madness, yet there is a method in it.

~ *William Shakespeare*

——— **INSECTS** ———

When the insects take over the world we hope they will remember, with gratitude, how we took them along on our picnics.   ~ *Bill Vaughn*

——— **INSIGHT** ———

You grow up the day you have the first real laugh at yourself.   ~ *Ethel Barrymore*

——— **INSINCERE** ———

The most exhausting thing in life is being insincere.

~ *Anne Morrow*
Lindbergh

——— **INSOMNIA** ———

Insomnia is the act of staying awake during chemistry class.

——— **INSPIRATION** ———

I don't know anything about inspiration because I

don't know what inspiration is; I've heard about it, but I never saw it.   ~ *William Faulkner*

—— INSTITUTION ——

An institution is the lengthened shadow of one man.   ~ *Ralph Waldo Emerson*

—— INSULT ——

The only graceful way to accept an insult is to ignore it; if you can't ignore it, top it; if you can't top it, laugh at it; if you can't laugh at it, it's probably deserved.   ~ *Russell Lynes*

The way to procure insults is to submit to them. A man meets with no more respect than he exacts.

~ *William Hazlitt*

Thou has added insult to injury.

~ *Phaedrus*

It is often better not to see an insult than to avenge it.   ~ *Seneca*

—— INTEGRITY ——

Better be poor and honest than rich and dishonest.

~ *Proverbs 19:1*

——— INTERFERE ———

Yanking a dog's ears is no more foolish than interfering in an argument that isn't any of your business.

~ Proverbs 26:17

——— INTIMATE ———

Two women seldom grow intimate but at the expense of a third person.   *~ Jonathan Swift*

——— INTOLERANCE ———

The devil loves nothing better than the intolerance of reformers.   *~ Lowell*

I hate intolerant people.

——— INTRUSIVENESS ———

The great secret of life is never to be in the way of others.   *~ T.C. Haliburton*

——— INVENTION ———

If a man can write a better book, or preach a better sermon, or build a better mousetrap than his neighbor, though he builds his house in the woods, the world will make a beaten path to his door.

~ Ralph Waldo Emerson

INVENTOR

I invent nothing. I rediscover.

~Auguste Rodin

INVESTMENT

I was shipwrecked before I got aboard.

~Seneca

The buck stopped before it got to me.

Hard work is the soundest investment. It provides a neat security for your widow's next husband.

IRRITATING

There is nobody so irritating as somebody with less intelligence and more sense than we have.

~Don Herold

JEALOUSY

In jealousy there is more self-love than love.

~Francois
de La Rochefoucauld

O jealousy! thou magnifier of trifles.

~Schiller

—— JEST ——

He that would jest must take a jest, else to let it alone were best.

Many a true word is spoke in jest.

~ *English Proverb*

—— JESUS CHRIST ——

Philosophical argument has sometimes shaken my reason for the faith that was in me; but my heart has always assured me that the Gospel of Jesus Christ must be reality. ~ *Daniel Webster*

Alexander, Caesar, Charlemagne, and myself found empires; but on what foundation did we rest the creations of our genius? Upon force. Jesus Christ founded an empire upon love; and at this hour millions of men would die for him. ~ *Napoleon*

It takes no brains to be an atheist. Any stupid person can deny the existence of a supernatural power because man's physical senses cannot detect it. But here cannot be ignored the influence of conscience, the respect we feel for moral law, the mystery of first life...or the marvelous order in which the universe moves about us on this earth. All these evidence the handiwork of the beneficent Deity. For my part that Deity is the God of the Bible and of Jesus Christ, his Son. ~ *Dwight D. Eisenhower*

—— JOKE ——

Take a joke as a joke, and it will not provoke.

It is no joke to bear with a man who is all jokes.

I don't make jokes. I just watch the government and report the facts.   *~ Will Rogers*

If Adam came on earth again, the only thing he would recognize would be the old jokes.

~ Thomas Dewar

—— JOY ——

One joy dispels a hundred cares.

~ Oriental Proverb

—— JUDGE ——

We are all inclined to judge ourselves by our ideals, others by their acts.   *~ Harold Nicholson*

Before I judge my neighbor, let me walk a mile in his moccasins.

Judge a tree from its fruit; not from the leaves.

~ Euripides

Examine the contents, not the bottle.

~ The Talmud

Judge a man by his questions rather than by his answers.   ~ *Voltaire*

Four things belong to a judge: to hear courteously, to answer wisely, to consider soberly, and to decide impartially.   ~ *Socrates*

——— JUDGMENT ———

One man's word is no man's word; we should quietly hear both sides.   ~ *Goethe*

Give your decision, never your reasons; your decisions may be right, your reasons are sure to be wrong.

~ *Lord Mansfield*

Every man prefers belief to the exercise of judgment.   ~ *Seneca*

Everyone should sweep before his own door.

Good judgment comes from experience; and experience, well, that comes from bad judgment.

Everyone complains of his memory, no one of his judgment.   ~ *Francois
de La Rochefoucauld*

——— JUNK ———

Junk is something you keep for years and then throw out two weeks before you need it.

——— JURY ———

A fox should not be the jury at a goose's trial.

~*Thomas Fuller*

A jury consists of twelve persons chosen to decide who has the better lawyer.   ~*Robert Frost*

——— JUST ———

People become house builders through building houses, harp players through playing the harp. We grow to be just by doing things which are just.

——— JUSTICE ———

Justice is truth in action. ~*Joseph Joubert*

Justice discards party, friendship, kindred, and is always, therefore, represented as blind.

~*Joseph Addison*

Injustice is relatively easy to bear; what stings is justice.   ~*H.L. Mencken*

——— KINDNESS ———

Kindness has converted more sinners than zeal, eloquence, or learning.   ~*Frederick W. Faber*

Constant kindness can accomplish much. As the sun makes ice melt, kindness causes misunderstanding, mistrust, and hostility to evaporate.

~ *Albert Schweitzer*

Never tire of loyalty and kindness. Hold these virtues tightly. Write them deep within your heart.

~ *Proverbs 3:3, 4*

Wise sayings often fall on barren ground; but a kind word is never thrown away.

~ *Sir Arthur Helps*

Kindness in words creates confidence. Kindness in thinking creates profoundness. Kindness in giving creates love.

Kindness makes a fellow feel good whether it's being done to him or by him.

~ *Frank A. Clark*

One can pay back the loan of gold, but one lies forever in debt to those who are kind.

~ *Malay Proverb*

Be kind. Remember everyone you meet is fighting a hard battle.   ~ *Harry Thompson*

One kind word can warm three winter months.

~ *Japanese Proverb*

Wherever there is a human being there is a chance for a kindness. ~ *Seneca*

Kindness is irresistible, be it but sincere and no mock smile or mask assumed. For what can the most unconscionable of men do to thee if thou persist in being kindly to him? ~ *Marcus Aurelius*

KISS

Some women blush when they are kissed; some call for the police; some swear; some bite. But the worst are those who laugh.

KNOWLEDGE

All knowledge has its origins in our perceptions.

~ *Leonardo da Vinci*

Never try to tell everything you know. It may take too short a time. ~ *Norman Ford*

Since we cannot know all that is to be known of everything, we ought to know a little about everything.

~ *Blaise Pascal*

We do not know one-millionth of one percent about anything. ~ *Thomas Edison*

Some students drink at the fountain of knowledge. Others just gargle

Those who think they know it all are very annoying to those of us who do. ~ *Robert K. Mueller*

The trouble with the world is not that people know too little, but that they know so many things that ain't so. ~ *Mark Twain*

A man who carries a cat by the tail learns something he can learn in no other way.

~ *Mark Twain*

Strange how much you've got to know before you know how little you know.

He that increaseth knowledge increaseth sorrow.

~ *Ecclesiastes 1:18 (KJV)*

Universities are full of knowledge; the freshmen bring a little in and the seniors take none away, and knowledge accumulates. ~ *Abbott Lowell*

——— **LANGUAGE** ———

The chief virtue that language can have is clearness, and nothing detracts from it so much as the use of unfamiliar words. ~ *Hippocrates*

Drawing on my fine command of language, I said nothing. ~ *Robert Benchley*

——— **LAUGHTER** ———

A hearty laugh gives one a dry cleaning, while a good cry is a wet wash.

If you're not allowed to laugh in heaven, I don't want to go there. ~ *Martin Luther*

No one is more profoundly sad than he who laughs too much. ~ *Jean Paul Richter*

A good laugh is sunshine in a house.

~ *William M. Thackeray*

Of all the things God created, I am often most grateful he created laughter.

~ *Charles Swindoll*

He who has learned how to laugh at himself shall never cease to be entertained.

~ *John Powell*

I want to make people laugh—so they will begin to see things seriously. ~ *William Zinsser*

He who laughs, lasts. ~ *Mary Pettibone Poole*

If any cleric or monk speaks jocular words, such as provoke laughter, let him be anathema.

~ *Ordinance, Second Council of Constance (1418)*

With the fearful strain that is on me night and day, if I did not laugh I should die. ~ *Abraham Lincoln*

Laughter is the shortest distance between two people. ~ *Victor Borge*

Laughter is the sensation of feeling good all over, and showing it principally in one place.

~ *Josh Billings*

Laugh and the world laughs with you, weep and you weep alone; for the sad old earth must borrow its mirth, but has trouble enough of its own.

~ *Ella Wheeler Wilcox*

LAW

We must reject the idea that every time a law is broken, society is guilty rather than the lawbreaker. It is time to restore the American precept that each individual is accountable for his actions.

~ *Ronald Reagan*

Laws too gentle are seldom obeyed; too severe, seldom executed. *~ Benjamin Franklin*

—— LAWYER ——

A lawyer is someone who helps you get what is coming to him.

Lawyers spend a great deal of their time shoveling smoke. *~ Oliver Wendell Holmes*

The first thing we do, let's kill all the lawyers.
~ William Shakespeare

Anybody who thinks talk is cheap should get some legal advice. *~ Franklin P. Jones*

—— LAZINESS ——

Laziness is the mother of invention.

To do nothing is in every man's power.
~ Samuel Johnson

Laziness grows on people; it begins in cobwebs and ends in iron chains. *~ M. Hale*

Laziness travels so slowly that poverty soon overtakes him.

——— LAZY ———

Take a lesson from the ants, you lazy fellow. Learn from their ways and be wise! For though they have no king to make them work, yet they labor hard all summer, gathering food for the winter. But you—all you do is sleep. When will you wake up?

~ Proverbs 6:6-9

A lazy man is brother to the saboteur.

~ Proverbs 18:9

The lazy man is full of excuses. "I can't go to work!" he says. "If I go outside I might meet a lion in the street and be killed!" *~ Proverbs 22:13*

The lazy man won't go out and work. "There might be a lion outside!" he says. He sticks to his bed like a door to its hinges! He is too tired even to lift his food from his dish to his mouth! Yet in his own opinion he is smarter than seven wise men.

~ Proverbs 26:13

He who has nothing to do has a real disadvantage: He can't stop and rest.

——— LEADERSHIP ———

Some must follow, and some command, though all are made of clay. *~ Henry Wadsworth Longfellow*

You do not lead by hitting people over the head—that's assault, not leadership.

~ *Dwight D. Eisenhower*

No man will ever be a big executive who feels that he must, either openly or under cover, follow up every order he gives and see that it is done—nor will he ever develop a capable assistant. ~ *John L. Mahin*

You can judge a leader by the size of the problems he tackles—people nearly always pick a problem their own size, and ignore or leave to others the bigger or smaller ones. ~ *Anthony Jay*

In order to be a leader a man must have followers. And to have followers, a man must have their confidence. Hence the supreme quality for a leader is unquestionably integrity. Without it, no real success is possible, no matter whether it is on a section gang, a football field, in an army or in an office. If a man's associates find him guilty of phoniness, if they find that he lacks forthright integrity, he will fail. His teachings and actions must square with each other. The first great need, therefore, is integrity and high purpose. ~ *Dwight D. Eisenhower*

Anyone can steer the ship when the sea is calm.

~ *Publilius Syrus*

He who cannot obey, cannot command.

~ *Benjamin Franklin*

——— LEARNING ———

Reading maketh a full man; conference a ready man; and writing an exact man.

~ *Francis Bacon*

Men learn while they teach.

~ *Seneca*

Wear your learning like your watch, in a private pocket; and do not pull it out and strike it, merely to show that you have one. ~ *Lord Chesterfield*

The three foundations of learning: seeing much, suffering much, and studying much.

~ *Caterall*

A little learning is a dangerous thing; drink deep, or taste not the Pierian spring; their shallow draughts intoxicate the brain, and drinking largely sobers us again. ~ *Alexander Pope*

——— LEAVING ———

It is amazing how nice people are to you when they know you are going away. ~ *Michael Arlen*

——— LEISURE ———

Only a person who can live with himself can enjoy the gift of leisure. ~ *Henry Greber*

The real problem with your leisure is how to keep other people from using it.

Leisure is the mother of philosophy.

~ *Thomas Hobbes*

—— **LENDING** ——

Unless you have the extra cash on hand, don't countersign a note. Why risk everything you own? They'll even take your bed! ~ *Proverbs 22:26, 27*

If you lend, you either lose the money or gain an enemy. ~ *Albanian Proverb*

—— **LETTER** ——

I have made this letter longer than usual because I lack the time to make it shorter.

~ *Blaise Pascal*

—— **LIAR** ——

A liar needs a good memory.

~ *Quintilian*

The biggest liar in the world is—They Say.

~ *Douglas Malloch*

I have nothing to hide. The White House has nothing to hide.   ~ *Richard M. Nixon*

The liar's punishment is not in the least that he is not believed but that he cannot believe anyone else.
                                    ~ *George Bernard Shaw*

No man has a good enough memory to be a successful liar.   ~ *Abraham Lincoln*

——— LIBERAL ———

I can remember way back when a liberal was one who was generous with his own money.
                                    ~ *Will Rogers*

One who has both feet firmly planted in the air.

——— LIBERTY ———

God grants liberty only to those who love it, and are always ready to guard it.   ~ *Daniel Webster*

Eternal vigilance is the price of liberty.
                                    ~ *Wendell Phillips*

Give me liberty, or give me death.
                                    ~ *Patrick Henry*

LIES

Sin has many tools, but a lie is the handle that fits them all.

Telling lies about someone is as harmful as hitting him with an axe, or wounding him with a sword, or shooting him with a sharp arrow.

~ Proverbs 25:18

The cruelest lies are often told in silence.

~ Robert Louis Stevenson

One of the striking differences between a cat and a lie is that the cat has only nine lives.

~ Mark Twain

Those that think it permissible to tell white lies soon grow color-blind.   *~ Austin O'Malley*

LIFE

Life not only begins at forty—it begins to show.

The first half of our life is ruined by our parents and the second half by our children.

~ Clarence Darrow

Life would be infinitely happier if we could only be born at the age of eighty and gradually approach eighteen.   *~ Mark Twain*

Life is an onion and one cries while peeling it.

~ *French Proverb*

Life is a continual process of getting used to things we never expected.   ~ *Bits and Pieces*

We make a living by what we get, but we make a life by what we give.   ~ *Norman MacEwan*

The trouble with life is that it is so daily.

No matter how bad things get you got to go on living, even if it kills you.   ~ *Sholem Aleichem*

Every man's life is a fairy tale written by God's fingers.   ~ *Hans Christian
Andersen*

We are always complaining that our days are few, and acting as though there would be no end to them.

~ *Seneca*

Life is easier to take than you'd think; all that is necessary is to accept the impossible, do without the indispensable, and bear the intolerable.

~ *Kathleen Norris*

Live each day as if it were your last—someday you'll be right.

No one is to be despaired of as long as he breathes. (While there is life there is hope.)

~ *Erasmus*

A useless life is an early death.

~ *Goethe*

I wish to preach not the doctrine of ignoble ease, but the doctrine of the strenuous life.

~ *Theodore Roosevelt*

As is a tale, so is life: not how long it is, but how good it is, is what matters. ~ *Seneca*

LIGHT

Better to light one small candle than to curse the darkness. ~ *Chinese Proverb*

We are told to let our light shine, and if it does, we won't need to tell anybody it does. Lighthouses don't fire cannons to call attention to their shining—they just shine. ~ *D.L. Moody*

LINCOLN

His heart was as great as the world, but there was no room in it to hold the memory of a wrong.

~ *Ralph Waldo Emerson*

—— LION ——

There may come a time when the lion and the lamb will lie down together, but I am still betting on the lion.

~ *Josh Billings*

It is not good to wake a sleeping lion.

~ *Philip Sidney*

—— LISTEN ——

It takes a great man to make a good listener.

~ *Sir Arthur Helps*

No man would listen to you talk if he didn't know it was his turn next. ~ *Edgar Watson Howe*

—— LISTENING ——

What a shame—yes, how stupid!—to decide before knowing the facts! ~ *Proverbs 18:13*

Nothing makes a person such a good listener as eavesdropping. ~ *Franklin P. Jones*

One of the best ways to persuade others is by listening to them. ~ *Dean Rusk*

From listening comes wisdom, and from speaking repentance.   *~ Italian Proverb*

A good listener is not only popular everywhere, but after a while he knows something.

~ Wilson Mizer

—— LITERATURE ——

In literature as in love, we are astonished at what is chosen by others.   *~ Andre Maurois*

—— LIVE ——

Let us endeavor so to live that when we come to die even the undertaker will be sorry.

—— LOAN ——

It is better to give than to lend, and it costs about the same.   *~ Philip Gibbs*

—— LOANS ——

It is risky to make loans to strangers!

~ Proverbs 20:16

—— LOGIC ——

Logic is like the sword—those who appeal to it shall perish by it. ~ *Samuel Butler*

Against logic there is no armor like ignorance.
~ *Lawrence Peter*

If you're strong on facts and weak on logic, talk facts; if you're strong on logic and weak on facts, talk logic. If you're weak on both, pound on the table.

—— LONELINESS ——

It is strange to be known so universally and yet to be so lonely. ~ *Albert Einstein*

In Genesis it says that it is not good for a man to be alone, but sometimes it is a great relief.

~ *John Barrymore*

—— LOS ANGELES ——

Los Angeles: A town where you can watch night baseball almost any afternoon.

~ *Changing Times*

—— LOSERS ——

He's a real loser. He moved into a new neighborhood and got run over by the Welcome Wagon.

~ Red Buttons

—— LOST ——

Many people get lost when trying to find an alternate route for the strait and narrow.

~ Good Reading

—— LOVE ——

Nothing raises man to such noble peaks nor drops him into such ashpits of absurdity as the act of falling in love. *~ Ridgely Hunt*

If Jack's in love, he's no judge of Jill's beauty.

~ Benjamin Franklin

Love is friendship set on fire.

~ Jeremy Taylor

Love does not die easily. It is a living thing. It thrives in the face of all life's hazards, save one—neglect.

~ James Bryden

Love and a cough cannot be hid.

~ George Herbert

Love will always find a way to be practical.

~ *Joe White*

Love is like the measles—all the worse when it comes late in life. ~ *Douglas Jerrold*

Love arrives on tiptoe and bangs the door when it leaves. ~ *Robert Lembke*

I love mankind—it's people I can't stand!

~ *Linus*

Love: A grave mental illness.

~ *Plato*

The heart has its reasons which reason does not understand. ~ *Blaise Pascal*

The way to a man's heart is through his stomach.

~ *Traditional Proverb*

To love and win is the best thing; to love and lose, the next best. ~ *William M. Thackeray*

Love never dies of starvation but often of indigestion. ~ *Ninon de Lenclos*

Love is the only fire against which there is no insurance.

Love is blind, and marriage is an eye-opener.

Love cures people—both the ones who give it and the ones who receive it.   *~ Dr. Karl Menninger*

In life, actions speak louder than words, but in love, the eyes do.   *~ Susan B. Anthony*

If you would be loved, be lovable.

~ Benjamin Franklin

The way to love anything is to realize that it might be lost.   *~ G.K. Chesterton*

Love is a softening of the hearteries.

Love is a fabric which never fades, no matter how often it is washed in the water of adversity and grief.

Love may not make the world go around, but it sure makes the trip worthwhile.

An old man in love is like a flower in winter.

~ Portuguese Proverb.

The heart that loves is always young.

Where there is great love there is great pain.

He drew a circle that shut me out, but love and I had the wit to win; we drew a larger circle that took him in.

The first sign of love is the last of wisdom.

~ Antoine Bret

There is no fear in love; but perfect love casteth out fear.   ~ *1 John 4:18* (KJV)

Greater love hath no man than this, that a man lay down his life for his friends.

~ *John 15:13* (KJV)

Everybody in love is blind.

~ *Propertius*

Better is a dinner of herbs where love is, than a stalled ox and hatred therewith.

~ *Proverbs 15:17* (KJV)

Love sought is good, but given unsought is better.

~ *William Shakespeare*

Some pray to marry the man they love, my prayer will somewhat vary: I humbly pray to heaven above that I love the man I marry. ~ *Rose Pastor Stokes*

You may talk all you please about patriotism and religion, but a right good love affair moves a man more than anything else.   ~ *Ed Howe*

Love is very patient and kind, never jealous or envious, never boastful or proud, never haughty or selfish or rude. Love does not demand its own way. It is not irritable or touchy. It does not hold grudges and will hardly even notice when others do it wrong. It is never glad about injustice, but rejoices whenever truth wins out. If you love someone you will be loyal to him no matter what the cost. You will always believe in him, always expect the best of him, and always stand your ground in defending him.   ~ *1 Corinthians 13:4-7*

There are three things that remain—faith, hope, and love—and the greatest of these is love.

~ *1 Corinthians 13:13*

——— LOYALTY ———

We are all in the same boat in a stormy sea, and we owe each other a terrible loyalty.

~ *G.K. Chesterton*

It is better to be faithful than famous.

~ *Theodore Roosevelt*

Often loyalty consists of keeping your mouth shut.

——— LUCK ———

I'm a great believer in luck and I find the harder I work the more I have of it.   ~ *Stephen Leacock*

—— LYING ——

A lie travels around the world while Truth is putting on her boots. ~ *Charles H. Spurgeon*

A liar is not believed even though he tells the truth. ~ *Cicero*

A good memory is needed once we have lied. ~ *Pierre Corneille*

Show me a liar, and I will show thee a thief. ~ *George Herbert*

That a lie which is half a truth is ever the blackest of lies; that a lie which is all a lie may be met and fought with outright—but a lie which is part a truth is a harder matter to fight. ~ *Lord Tennyson*

—— MAD ——

Man is certainly stark mad; he cannot make a worm, and yet he will be making gods by dozens. ~ *Michel de Montaigne*

When you see a married couple coming down the street, the one who is two or three steps ahead is the one that's mad. ~ *Helen Rowland*

MAJORITY

If fifty million people say a foolish thing it is still a foolish thing.
~ *Anatole France*

MALICE

Malice drinks its own poison.

MAN

If you can dream and not make dreams your
master.
If you can think and not make thoughts your
aim;
If you can meet with triumph and disaster;
And treat those two imposters just the same,
If you can force your heart, and nerve, and sinew
To serve your turn long after they are gone;
And so hold on when there is nothing in you
Except the will which says to them, "Hold on,"
If you can fill the unforgiving minute
With sixty seconds' worth of distance run,
Yours is the earth and everything that's in it,
And, what is more, you'll be a man, my son.

~ *Rudyard Kipling*

Man's inhumanity to man makes countless thousands mourn!
~ *Robert Burns*

Men are the only animals that devote themselves, day in and day out, to making one another unhappy.

~ *H.L. Mencken*

MANAGEMENT

So much of what we call management consists in making it difficult for people to work.

~ *Peter Drucker*

MANNERS

Manners are the happy ways of doing things.

~ *Ralph Waldo Emerson*

One learns manners from those who have none.

MANUSCRIPT

A manuscript, like a fetus, is never improved by showing it to somebody before it is completed.

Your manuscript is both good and original; but the part that is good is not original, and the part that is original is not good.   ~ *Samuel Johnson*

Manuscript: Something submitted in haste and returned at leisure. ~*Oliver Herford*

MARIJUANA

Sometimes I'm asked by kids why I condemn marijuana when I haven't tried it. The greatest obstetricians in the world have never been pregnant.

~*Art Linkletter*

MARRIAGE

Often the difference between a successful marriage and a mediocre one consists of leaving about three or four things a day unsaid. ~*Harlan Miller*

To keep your marriage brimming,
With love in the loving cup,
Whenever you're wrong, admit it,
Whenever you're right, shut up.

~*Ogden Nash*

I have done thousands of hours of marriage counseling, and yet, I have never seen two unselfish people ever get a divorce. I never have had anyone rush into my office and say, "I want out of this marriage. My spouse has been too good and too nice to me."

~*R.E. Phillips*

He who marries for money earns it.

~ *Hebrew Proverb*

Keep thy eyes wide open before marriage, and half shut afterward.   ~ *Thomas Fuller*

A good marriage would be between a blind wife and a deaf husband.   ~ *Michel de Montaigne*

Strange to say what delight we married people have to see these poor fools decoyed into our condition.

~ *Samuel Pepys*

Marriage resembles a pair of shears, so joined that they cannot be separated; often moving in opposite directions, yet always punishing anyone who comes between them.   ~ *Sydney Smith*

By all means marry; if you get a good wife, you'll become happy; if you get a bad one, you'll become a philosopher.   ~ *Socrates*

A successful marriage is one in which you fall in love many times, always with the same person.

~ *McLaughlin*

It is better for a woman to marry a man who loves her than a man she loves.   ~ *Arab Proverb*

Thus grief still treads upon the heels of pleasure, marry in haste, we may repent at leisure.

~ *William Congreve*

Matrimony: The high sea for which no compass has yet been invented.   ~ *Heinrich Heine*

When the blind lead the blind, they both fall into matrimony.   ~ *George Farquhar*

—— MARTYR ——

The tyrant dies and his rule ends, the martyr dies and his rule begins.   ~ *Soren Kierkegaard*

—— MEDICINE ——

God heals and the doctor takes the fee.

~ *Benjamin Franklin*

—— MEEK ——

It's going to be fun to watch and see how long the meek can keep the earth after they inherit it.

~ *Kin Hubbard*

It's too bad that the meek haven't already inherited the earth, because the unmeek are making a real mess of it.

——— MEMORIES ———

God gave us our memories so that we might have roses in December.   ~*James Barrie*

Let us not burden our remembrances with a heaviness that is gone.   ~*William Shakespeare*

A retentive memory is a good thing, but the ability to forget is the true token of greatness.

~*Elbert Hubbard*

When I was younger I could remember anything, whether it had happened or not.

~*Mark Twain*

The advantage of a bad memory is that one enjoys several times the same good things for the first time.

~*Friedrich Nietzsche*

When waiting for old age, be sure to put away a few pleasant thoughts.

I used to have trouble remembering names till I took that Sam Carnegie course.

~*Jack Taylor*

You never realize what a good memory you have until you try to forget something.

If you tell the truth, you don't have to remember anything.   ~*Mark Twain*

I've a grand memory for forgetting.

~ *Robert Louis Stevenson*

No man has a good enough memory to make a successful liar. ~ *Abraham Lincoln*

Why can we remember the tiniest detail that has happened to us, and not remember how many times we have told it to the same persons?

~ *Francois
de La Rochefoucauld*

The creditor hath a better memory than the debtor.

~ *James Howell*

—— **MEN** ——

An important difference between men and women is that women are smarter than men about women.

God give us men. A time like this demands strong minds, great hearts, true faith, and ready hands! Men whom the lust of office does not kill, men whom the spoils of office cannot buy, men who possess opinions and a will, men who love honor, men who cannot lie.

~ *J.G. Holland*

—— **MENTAL ILLNESS** ——

There are more men than women in mental hospitals, which just goes to show who's driving who crazy.

~ *Peter Veale*

—— MENU ——

As a child my family's menu consisted of two choices: take it, or leave it. ~*Buddy Hackett*

—— METHOD ——

There nearly always is method in madness. It's what drives men mad, being methodical.

~*G.K. Chesterton*

—— MIDDLE AGE ——

Middle age is when your age starts to show around your middle. ~*Bob Hope*

Middle age is when you're sitting at home on Saturday night and the telephone rings and you hope it isn't for you. ~*Ogden Nash*

Middle age is when your old classmates are so grey and wrinkled and bald they don't recognize you.

~*Bennet Cerf*

Middle age is when you've met so many people that every new person you meet reminds you of someone else. ~*Ogden Nash*

Life begins at 40—but so do fallen arches, lumbago, faulty eyesight, and the tendency to tell a story to the same person three or four times.

~*Bill Feather*

You've reached middle age when people begin to recognize you from the rear, too.

Middle age is when everything starts to click—your elbows, knees, and neck.   ~*Robert Orben*

———— **MIND** ————

How many of you are like me? You like to speak to see what you have on your mind.

At a certain age some people's minds close up; they live on their intellectual fat. ~*William Lyon Phelps*

The mind is its own place and in itself can make a heaven of hell, a hell of heaven.

~*John Milton*

———— **MINISTER** ————

The minister's brain is often the "poor-box" of the church.   ~*Whipple*

———— **MIRACLE** ————

A modern miracle would be a golden wedding anniversary in Hollywood.

——— MISCOMMUNICATION ———

All miscommunication is the result of differing assumptions.

——— MISER ———

Misers aren't fun to live with, but they make wonderful ancestors.   *~ David Brenner*

——— MISERABLE ———

The secret of being miserable is to have the leisure to bother about whether you are happy or not.

~ George Bernard Shaw

——— MISERY ———

Misery loves company.   *~ English Proverb*

Fire tries gold, misery tries brave men.

~ Seneca

He that is down need fear no fall.

~ John Bunyan

——— MISFORTUNE ———

We all have enough strength to bear the misfortunes of others.   *~ Francois*
de La Rochefoucauld

If all our misfortunes were laid in one common heap, whence everyone must take an equal portion, most people would be contented to take their own and depart. ~ *Solon*

Great minds have purposes, others have wishes. Little minds are tamed and subdued by misfortune; but great minds rise above them.

~ *Washington Irving*

The measure of a man is the way he bears up under misfortune. ~ *Plutarch*

Let us be of good cheer, remembering that the misfortunes hardest to bear are those which never happen. ~ *James Russell Lowell*

The worst misfortune that can happen to an ordinary man is to have an extraordinary father.

~ *Austin O'Malley*

——— **MISTAKE** ———

A mistake at least proves somebody stopped talking long enough to do something.

Learn from the mistakes of others—you can never live long enough to make them all yourself.

A man who refuses to admit his mistakes can never be successful. But if he confesses and forsakes them, he gets another chance. ~*Proverbs 28:13*

If you must make mistakes, it will be more to your credit if you make a new one each time.

——— MISTRUST ———

When mistrust enters, love departs.

——— MISUNDERSTANDING ———

Is it so bad, then, to be misunderstood? Pythagoras was misunderstood, and Socrates, and Jesus, and Luther, and Copernicus, and Galileo, and Newton, and every pure and wise spirit that ever took flesh. To be great is to be misunderstood.

~*Ralph Waldo Emerson*

——— MOCKER ———

Throw out the mocker, and you will be rid of tension, fighting and quarrels. ~*Proverbs 22:10*

——— MODESTY ———

A modest man never talks of himself.

~*Jean de La Bruyere*

——— MONDAY ———

Monday is a terrible way to spend one-seventh of your life. *~Houghton Line*

——— MONEY ———

When I have any money I get rid of it as quickly as possible, lest it find a way into my heart.

~John Wesley

The safest way to double your money is to fold it over once and put it in your pocket.

*~Frank McKinney
Hubbard*

That money talks
I'll not deny,
I heard it once:
It said, "Goodbye."

~Richard Armour

Money is a terrible master but an excellent servant.

~P.T. Barnum

If you would know what the Lord God thinks of money, you have only to look at those to whom he gives it. *~Maurice Baring*

It's peculiar how a dollar can look so big when it goes to church and so small when it goes for groceries.

~Grit

Never lend money to a friend. It's dangerous—it could damage his memory. ~ *Sam Levenson*

To figure your cost of living simply take your income and add 10 percent.

Today women often push carts through supermarkets at speeds over $65 an hour.

~ *Joseph Salak*

There is only one thing money won't buy, and that's poverty. ~ *Joe E. Lewis*

If you would know the value of money, go and try to borrow some. ~ *Benjamin Franklin*

If you would lose a troublesome visitor, lend him money. ~ *Benjamin Franklin*

Every crowd has a silver lining.

~ *P.T. Barnum*

Money is the fruit of evil as often as the root of it.

~ *Henry Fielding*

Just about the time you think you can make both ends meet, somebody moves the ends.

Spend less than you get.

If your outgo exceeds your income, then your upkeep will be your downfall.

A fool and his money are soon parted.

~ *George Buchanan*

When money speaks, the truth is silent.

~ *Russian Proverb*

The love of money is the root of all evil.

~ *1 Timothy 6:10* (KJV)

—— MOOD ——

We have absolutely no right to annoy others by our various moods. Let the prevailing mood be cheerful and serene; keep your other moods to yourself, or better still, get rid of them. ~ *Anne Gould*

—— MORALITY ——

The new morality is terrible. It's taken all the sting out of gossip.

To give a man full knowledge of true morality, I would send him to no other book than the New Testament. ~ *John Locke*

—— MORNING ——

The early morning has gold in its mouth.

~ *Benjamin Franklin*

———— MOTHERS ————

An ounce of mother is worth more than a pound of clergy.   *~H.H. Birkins*

God could not be everywhere, and therefore he made mothers.   *~ Hebrew Proverb*

———— MOTIVATION ————

Motivation is what gets you started. Habit is what keeps you going.   *~Jim Ryun*

People are always motivated by at least two reasons: the one they tell you about, and a secret one.

~O.A. Batista

———— MOTIVES ————

We can justify our every deed but God looks at our motives.   *~Proverbs 21:2*

———— MOUTH ————

Keep your mouth closed and you'll stay out of trouble.   *~Proverbs 21:23*

Be sure your brain is in gear before engaging your mouth.

MURDER

Every unpunished murder takes away something from the security of every man's life.

~Daniel Webster

MUSIC

Music hath charms to soothe the savage beast.

~James Bramston

Music hath charm to soothe a savage beast—but I'd try a revolver first.   *~Josh Billings*

NECESSITY

Necessity is the mother of invention.

~Latin Proverb

NEEDS

You never know what you can do without until you try.   *~Franklin Pierce Adams*

NEIGHBOR

No one is rich enough to do without a neighbor.

~Danish Proverb

When your neighbor's house is afire your own property is at stake.   ~*Horace*

——— **NERVOUS BREAKDOWN** ———

One of the symptoms of an approaching nervous breakdown is the belief that one's work is terribly important.   ~*Bertrand Russell*

——— **NEUTRALITY** ———

The hottest places in hell are reserved for those who in time of great moral crises maintain their neutrality.

~*Dante*

——— **NEWSPAPER** ———

If newspapers are useful in overthrowing tyrants, it is only to establish a tyranny of their own.

~*James Fenimore Cooper*

I fear three newspapers more than a hundred thousand bayonets.   ~*Napoleon*

——— **NICE** ———

This would be a great world if everyone was as nice to you as the guy who's trying to sell you something.

~*Bits and Pieces*

Be nice to people on your way up because you'll meet them on your way down.

~ *Wilson Mizner*

NO

Learn to say no; it will be of more use to you than to be able to read Latin. ~ *Charles H. Spurgeon*

NOAH

Such is the human race. Often it does seem such a pity that Noah...didn't miss the boat.

~ *Mark Twain*

NOISE

Noise proves nothing; often a hen who has merely laid an egg cackles as if she had laid an asteroid.

~ *Mark Twain*

NONCONFORMITY

If there is anything the nonconformist hates worse than a conformist, it's another nonconformist who doesn't conform to the prevailing standards of nonconformity. ~ *Bill Vaughan*

Comedy is the last refuge of the nonconformist mind.   ~ *Gilbert Seldes*

——— NONSENSE ———

A little nonsense now and then is relished by the wisest men.

——— NOTHING ———

The only thing necessary for the triumph of evil is for good men to do nothing.

~ *Edmund Burke*

——— NOVEL ———

There are three rules for writing a novel. Unfortunately, no one knows what they are.

~ *W. Somerset Maugham*

Every novel should have a beginning, a muddle, and an end.   ~ *Peter de Vries*

The great American novel has not only already been written, it has already been rejected.

~ *Frank Dane*

——— OATH ———

A liar freely gives his oath.

~ *Pierre Corneille*

OBEDIENCE

Every great person has first learned how to obey, whom to obey, and when to obey.

~ William Ward

OBNOXIOUS

I don't know what makes him so obnoxious. But whatever it is, it works. *~ Goddard*

OFFEND

It is harder to win back the friendship of an offended brother than to capture a fortified city. His anger shuts you out like iron bars.

~ Proverbs 18:19

OLD AGE

Of late I appear
To have reached that stage
When people look old
Who are only my age.

~ Richard Armour

You know you're getting old when the candles cost more than the cake. *~ Bob Hope*

If I'd known I was going to live so long, I'd have taken better care of myself. ~ *Leon Eldred*

First you forget names, then you forget faces, then you forget to pull your zipper up, then you forget to pull your zipper down. ~ *Leo Rosenberg*

I am in the prime of senility.

~ *Joel Chandler Harris*

As soon as you feel too old to do a thing, go out and do it. As soon as you feel critical, say something kind in a kindly way. As soon as you feel neglected, send a cheery note to a friend. ~ *Oliver Wilson*

The older we get the less we are sure that the man who disagrees with us is a bigot, a moron, or a scoundrel. We even suspect that he may be as close to being right as we are.

Every man desires to live long, but no man would be old. ~ *Jonathan Swift*

To me, old age is always fifteen years older than I am. ~ *Bernard Baruch*

Old age isn't so bad ... when you consider the alternative.

——— OPENNESS ———

Keep an open mind, but don't keep it too open or people will throw a lot of rubbish into it.

If you come at me with your fists doubled, I think I can promise you that mine will double as fast as yours; but if you come to me and say, "Let us sit down and take counsel together, and, if we differ from one another, understand why it is we differ from one another, just what the points at issue are," we will presently find that we are not so far apart after all, that the points on which we differ are few and the points on which we agree are many, and that if we only have the patience and the candor and the desire to get together, we will get together. ~ *Woodrow Wilson*

Stop a minute to contrast your keen interest in your own affairs with your mild concern about anything else. Realize then, that everybody else in the world feels exactly the same way! Then, along with Lincoln and Roosevelt, you will have grasped the only solid foundation for any job other than warden in a penitentiary; namely, that success in dealing with people depends on a sympathetic grasp of the other man's viewpoint. ~ *Kenneth M. Goode*

——— OPINION ———

It is not best that we should all think alike; it is difference of opinion which makes horse races.

~ *Mark Twain*

The pressure of public opinion is like the pressure of the atmosphere; you can't see it—but, all the same, it is sixteen pounds to the square inch.

~ *James Russell Lowell*

You can please some of the people some of the time; you can please all of the people some of the time; but you can never please all the people all the time.

~ *Abraham Lincoln*

New opinions are always suspected, and usually opposed, without any other reason but because they are not already common.   ~ *John Locke*

——— OPPORTUNITY ———

Opportunity is missed by most people because it is dressed in overalls and looks like work.

~ *Thomas Edison*

Our ship would come in much sooner if we'd swim out to meet it.

Opportunities multiply as they are seized; they die when neglected.

A man must make his opportunity as oft as find it.

~ *Francis Bacon*

The reason so many people never get anywhere in life is because, when opportunity knocks, they are out in the backyard looking for four-leaf clovers.

~ *Walter P. Chrysler*

To each is given a bag of tools,
A shapeless mass, and a book of rules,

And each must make, ere life is flown,
A stumbling-block or a stepping-stone.

When one door closes, another opens; but we often look so long and so regretfully upon the closed door that we do not see the one which has opened for us.

~ *Alexander Graham Bell*

Four things come not back—the spoken word, the sped arrow, the past life, and the neglected opportunity. ~ *Arab Proverb*

When written in Chinese, the word "crisis" is composed of two characters—one represents danger and the other represents opportunity.

~ *John F. Kennedy*

Gentlemen, we're surrounded by insurmountable opportunities. ~ *Pogo*

I'll study and get ready and be prepared for my opportunity when it comes. ~ *Abraham Lincoln*

The secret of success in life is for a man to be ready for his opportunity when it comes.

~ *Benjamin Disraeli*

The trouble with opportunity is that it is always more recognizable going than coming.

Ability is nothing without opportunity.

~ *Napoleon*

I always tried to turn every disaster into an opportunity. ~ *John D. Rockefeller*

Do you see difficulties in every opportunity or opportunities in every difficulty?

—— OPTIMISM ——

Some people are always grumbling because roses have thorns; I am thankful that thorns have roses.

~ *Alphonse Karr*

An optimist may see a light where there is none, but why must the pessimist always run to blow it out?

~ *Michel de Saint-Pierre*

An optimist is a fellow who believes a housefly is looking for a way to get out.

~ *George Nathan*

No man ever injured his eyesight by looking on the bright side of things.

—— ORATORY ——

When Demosthenes was asked what were the three most important aspects of oratory, he answered, "Action, Action, Action." ~ *Plutarch*

—— ORIGINALITY ——

Originality is the art of concealing your source.
> ~*Franklin P. Jones*

For I fear I have nothing original in me—except Original Sin.
> ~*Thomas Campbell*

—— OTHERS ——

It is when we forget ourselves that we do things that are most likely to be remembered.

Whatever you may be sure of, be sure of this, that you are dreadfully like other people.
> ~*James Russell Lowell*

Unless life is lived for others, it is not worthwhile.
> ~*Mother Teresa*

Talk to a man about himself and he will listen for hours.
> ~*Benjamin Disraeli*

—— OUTLOOK ——

If the only tool you have is a hammer, you tend to see every problem as a nail.

Reflect upon your present blessings, of which every man has plenty; not on your past misfortunes, of which all men have some. *~ Charles Dickens*

─── OVEREATING ───

An overeater is one who digs his grave with his teeth.

─── OWNERSHIP ───

The buck stops here. *~ Harry S. Truman*

─── PAIN ───

The real problem is not why some pious, humble, believing people suffer, but why some do not.

~ C.S. Lewis

Pain is an energy monster; we give it the power to hurt us. And we can take that power away—depending on how we choose to view ourselves. All pain is real, but you can change your reality.

~ David Black

─── PARENTS ───

Parents are the last people on earth who ought to have children. *~ Samuel Butler*

Train up a child in the way he should go—and walk there yourself once in a while.

~ *Josh Billings*

Do not handicap your children by making their lives easy.   ~ *Robert Heinlein*

—— PAST ——

It's futile to talk too much about the past—something like trying to make birth control retroactive.

~ *Charles E. Wilson*

The past is but the beginning of a beginning.

~ *H.G. Wells*

The past always looks better than it was; it's only pleasant because it isn't here.

~ *Finley P. Dunne*

Never worry about anything that is past. Charge it up to experience and forget the trouble. There are always plenty of troubles ahead, so don't turn and look back on any behind you.   ~ *Herbert Hoover*

That which is past is gone and irrevocable, and wise men have enough to do with things present and to come; therefore they do but trifle with themselves that labor in past matters.   ~ *Francis Bacon*

When a thing is done, it's done. Don't look back. Look forward to your next objective.

All the king's horses and all the king's men can't put the past together again. So let's remember: Don't try to saw sawdust.   ~ *Dale Carnegie*

——— PATIENCE ———

Be patient and you will finally win, for a soft tongue can break hard bones.   ~ *Proverbs 25:15*

Prayer of the modern American: "Dear God, I pray for patience. And I want it right now!"

~ *Oren Arnold*

Patience often gets the credit that belongs to fatigue.

An ounce of patience is worth a pound of brains.

Young folks should cultivate patience with old folks so that when they grow old they'll have patience with young folks.

Patience is a most necessary qualification for business; many a man would rather you heard his story than granted his request.   ~ *Lord Chesterfield*

One moment of patience may ward off great disaster; one moment of impatience may ruin a whole life.

~ *Chinese Proverb*

Patience is something you admire in the driver behind you, but not in the one ahead.

~ *Bill McGlashen*

If we would like to develop more patience, we should prepare for trouble. ~ *R.E. Phillips*

Everything comes to him who hustles while he waits. ~ *Thomas Edison*

Patience is the best remedy for every trouble.

~ *Plautus*

Lack of pep is often mistaken for patience.

~ *Frank Hubbard*

The secret of patience is doing something else in the meanwhile.

PATRIOTISM

I only regret that I have but one life to lose for my country. ~ *Nathan Hale*

And so, my fellow Americans, ask not what your country can do for you; ask what you can do for your country. ~ *John F. Kennedy*

I venture to suggest that patriotism is not a short and frenzied outburst of emotion but the tranquil and steady dedication of a lifetime.

~ *Adlai Stevenson*

——— PEACE ———

Peace is the deliberate adjustment of my life to the will of God.

Have courage for the great sorrows of life and patience for the small ones; and when you have laboriously accomplished your daily task, go to sleep in peace. God is awake. *~ Victor Hugo*

——— PEN ———

The pen is mightier than the sword.

~ Edward Bulwer-Lytton

——— PEOPLE ———

Too bad that all the people who know how to run the country are busy driving taxicabs and cutting hair.

~ George Burns

All mankind is divided into three classes: those that are immovable, those that are movable, and those that move.

~ Benjamin Franklin

——— PERFECTION ———

A perfectionist is one who takes great pains—and gives them to other people.

——— PERSEVERANCE ———

Every calling is great when greatly pursued.

~ *Oliver Wendell Holmes*

Victory belongs to the most persevering.

~ *Napoleon*

——— PERSISTENCE ———

Little strokes fell great oaks.

Feather by feather the goose is plucked.

~ *John Ray*

Nothing in the world can take the place of persistence. Talent will not; nothing is more common than unsuccessful men with talent. Genius will not; unrewarded genius is almost a proverb. Education will not; the world is full of educated derelicts. Persistence and determination alone are omnipotent. The slogan "Press on" has solved and always will solve the problems of the human race.   ~ *Calvin Coolidge*

It has been my observation that most people get ahead during the time that others waste.

——— PERSPIRATION ———

Genius is one percent inspiration and ninety-nine percent perspiration.   ~*Thomas Edison*

——— PERSUASION ———

I sit here all day trying to persuade people to do the things they ought to have sense enough to do without my persuading them. That's all the powers of the President amount to.   ~*Harry S. Truman*

Few are open to conviction, but the majority of men are open to persuasion.   ~*Goethe*

——— PESSIMISM ———

A pessimist is one who feels bad when he feels good for fear he'll feel worse when he feels better.

A pessimist? A man who thinks everybody is nasty as himself, and hates them for it.

~*George Bernard Shaw*

There is no sadder sight than a young pessimist.

~*Mark Twain*

Pessimist: One who, when he has the choice of two evils, chooses both.   ~*Oscar Wilde*

—— **PET PEEVE** ——

When a man has a "pet peeve" it's remarkable how often he pets it.

—— **PHILADELPHIA** ——

I once spent a year in Philadelphia. I think it was on a Sunday.   *~ W.C. Fields*

—— **PHILOSOPHY** ——

To be a real philosopher one must be able to laugh at philosophy.   *~ Blaise Pascal*

I've developed a new philosophy...I only dread one day at a time.   *~ Charlie Brown*

—— **PHYSICIAN** ——

Every physician almost hath his favorite disease.
                    ~ Henry Fielding

I am dying with the help of too many physicians.
                    ~ Alexander the Great

—— PLAGIARISM ——

When a thing has been said and said well, have no scruple. Take it and copy it. ~*Anatole France*

Taking something from one man and making it worse is plagiarism. ~*George Moore*

There is much difference between imitating a man and counterfeiting him. ~*Benjamin Franklin*

What a good thing Adam had. When he said a good thing, he knew nobody had said it before.
~*Mark Twain*

Originality is undetected plagiarism.
~*William R. Inge*

Genius borrows nobly. ~*Ralph Waldo Emerson*

Nothing is said which has not been said before.
~*Terence*

—— PLAIN ——

God must have loved the plain people; he made so many of them. ~*Abraham Lincoln*

PLANNING

When you're dying of thirst, it's too late to think about digging a well. *~Japanese Proverb*

PLANS

Don't brag about your plans for tomorrow—wait and see what happens. *~Proverbs 27:1*

Our plans miscarry because they have no aim. When a man does not know what harbor he is making for, no wind is the right wind.

~Seneca

PLAYS

He writes his plays for the ages—the ages between five and twelve. *~George Nathan*

PLEASANTNESS

It is easier to catch flies with honey than with vinegar. *~English Proverb*

PLEASE

If you please God, it doesn't matter whom you displease. If you displease God, it doesn't matter whom you please.

He who tries to please everybody will die before his time.

——— PLEASURE ———

There is no pleasure in having nothing to do; the fun is in having lots to do and not doing it.

~ *Mary Wilson Little*

——— POETRY ———

Publishing a volume of verse is like dropping a rose petal down the Grand Canyon and waiting for the echo. ~ *Don Marquis*

——— POLICY ———

When policy fails try thinking.

~ *American Proverb*

——— POLITICIAN ———

An honest politician is one who, when he is bought, will stay bought. ~ *Simon Cameron*

Too bad ninety percent of the politicians give the other ten percent a bad reputation.

~ *Henry Kissinger*

The famous politician was trying to save both his faces.
~ *John Gunther*

——— POLITICS ———

Politics are almost as exciting as war, and quite as dangerous. In war you can only be killed once, but in politics many times.
~ *Winston Churchill*

Politics is not a bad profession. If you succeed there are many rewards, if you disgrace yourself you can always write a book.
~ *Ronald Reagan*

Politics is perhaps the only profession for which no preparation is thought necessary.
~ *Robert Louis Stevenson*

All political parties die at last of swallowing their own lies.
~ *John Arbuthnot*

——— POOR ———

When you help the poor you are lending to the Lord—and he pays wonderful interest on your loan!
~ *Proverbs 19:17*

Not he who has little, but he who wishes more, is poor.
~ *Seneca*

—— POPULATION ——

We all worry about the population explosion—but we don't worry about it at the right time.

~ *Arthur Hoppe*

—— POSITIVE ——

There is no danger of developing eyestrain from looking on the bright side of things.

—— POTENTIAL ——

Treat people as if they were what they ought to be and to help them to become what they are capable of being.　　　~ *Goethe*

—— POVERTY ——

Poverty is uncomfortable; but nine times out of ten the best thing that can happen to a young man is to be tossed overboard and be compelled to sink or swim.

~ *James A. Garfield*

Poverty is not dishonorable in itself, but only when it comes from idleness, intemperance, extravagance, and folly.　　　~ *Plutarch*

POWER

Power intoxicates men. When a man is intoxicated by alcohol he can recover, but when intoxicated by power; he seldom recovers. *~James F. Byrnes*

The measure of man is what he does with power.

~Pittacus

Power may justly be compared to a great river; while kept within its bounds it is both beautiful and useful, but when it overflows its banks, it is then too impetuous to be stemmed; it bears down all before it, and brings destruction and desolation wherever it comes. *~Andrew Hamilton*

Whenever a man has cast a longing eye on offices, a rottenness begins in his conduct.

~Thomas Jefferson

Power tends to corrupt; absolute power corrupts absolutely. *~Lord Acton*

Give me a lever long enough and a prop strong enough, I can single-handed move the world.

~Archimedes

Patience and gentleness is power.

~Leigh Hunt

Unlimited power corrupts the possessor.

~William Pitt

He who has great power should use it lightly.

~ *Seneca*

——— PRAISE ———

The purity of silver and gold can be tested in a crucible, but a man is tested by his reaction to men's praise. ~ *Proverbs 27:21*

A bit of fragrance always clings to the hand that gives you roses. ~ *Chinese Proverb*

One thing scientists have discovered is that often-praised children become more intelligent than often-blamed ones. If some of your employees are a bit dumb, perhaps your treatment of them is to blame. There's a creative element in praise.

~ *Thomas Dreier*

He who gets someone else to blow his horn will find that the sound travels twice as far.

Praise, like gold and diamonds, owes its value to its scarcity.

The sweetest of all sounds is praise.

~ *Xenophon*

Don't praise yourself; let others do it!

~ *Proverbs 27:2*

Let another man praise thee, and not thine own mouth.   *~Proverbs 27:2* (KJV)

——— PRAYER ———

I have been driven many times to my knees by the overwhelming conviction that I had nowhere else to go. My own wisdom, and that of all about me, seemed insufficient for the day.   *~Abraham Lincoln*

Prayer does not change God, but changes him who prays.   *~Soren Kierkegaard*

——— PREACHING ———

He charged nothing for his preaching, and it was worth it, too.   *~Mark Twain*

——— PRECEPT ———

To do each day two things one dislikes is a precept I have followed scrupulously: Every day I have got up and I have gone to bed.   *~William Somerset Maugham*

——— PREFERENCE ———

Giving preferred treatment to rich people is a clear case of selling one's soul for a piece of bread.

~Proverbs 28:21

——— PREJUDICE ———

Opinions founded on prejudice are always sustained with the greatest violence.

~ *Francis Jeffery*

Prejudice is the ink with which all history is written.

~ *Mark Twain*

He hears but half who hears one party only.

~ *Aeschylus*

——— PREPAREDNESS ———

To be prepared for war is one of the most effectual means of preserving peace. ~ *George Washington*

——— PRESENTATION ———

A person will accept or reject your proposal in the first nine minutes of your presentation.

——— PRESIDENT ———

When I was a boy I was told that anyone could be president. I'm beginning to believe it.

~ *Clarence Darrow*

——— PRESSURE ———

He who rides a tiger is afraid to dismount.

~Chinese Proverb

——— PRETENDING ———

The only good in pretending is the fun we get out of fooling ourselves that we fool somebody.

~Booth Tarkington

——— PRIDE ———

Pride is the only disease known to man that makes everyone sick except the one who has it.

~Buddy Robinson

Pride goes before destruction and haughtiness before a fall. *~Proverbs 16:18*

When a man is wrapped up in himself, he makes a pretty small package. *~John Ruskin*

There is a paradox in pride: It makes some men ridiculous, but prevents others from becoming so.

~Charles Colton

Lord...where we are wrong, make us willing to change, and where we are right, make us easy to live with. *~Peter Marshall*

God made us, and God is able to empower us to do whatever he calls us to do. Denying that we can accomplish God's work is not humility; it is the worst kind of pride.   ~*Warren Wiersbe*

He who pats himself on the back may dislocate his shoulder.

He who gets on a high horse is riding for a fall.

He who is all wrapped up in himself is overdressed.

Most men are like eggs, too full of themselves to hold anything else.   ~*Josh Billings*

—— PRINCIPLES ——

Prosperity is the best protector of principle.
                    ~*Mark Twain*

When a fellow says it ain't the money but the principle of the thing, it's the money. ~*Kin Hubbard*

Important principles may and must be flexible.
                    ~*Abraham Lincoln*

It is easier to fight for one's principles than to live up to them.   ~*Alfred Adler*

——— PROBLEM ———

If you keep your head when all about you are losing theirs, you don't understand the problem.

A problem well-stated is a problem half-solved.
> ~*Charles F. Kettering*

——— PROBLEMS ———

The toughest years in life are those between ten and seventy. ~*Helen Hayes*

We live in the midst of alarms; anxiety clouds the future; we expect some new disaster with each newspaper we read. ~*Abraham Lincoln*

Has any man ever obtained inner harmony by simply reading about the experiences of others? Not since the world began has it ever happened. Each man must go through the fire himself.

> ~*Norman Douglas*

Having problems may not be so bad. We have a special place for folks who have none—it's called a cemetery. ~*Frank A. Clark*

Adolescence and snowdrifts are about the only problems that disappear if you ignore them long enough. ~*Wall Street Journal*

Most people spend more time and energy going around problems than in trying to solve them.

~ *Henry Ford*

Every problem contains within itself the seeds of its own solution. ~ *Bits and Pieces*

Charles Kettering, the inventor, had a unique method of solving problems. He would break down each problem into the smallest possible subproblems. Then he did research to find out which subproblems had already been solved. He often found that what looked like a huge problem had previously been 98 percent solved by other people. Then he tackled what was left. ~ *Bits and Pieces*

The best way to forget your own problems is to help someone else solve his.

Problems are only opportunities in work clothes.

~ *Henry J. Kaiser*

How insignificant this will appear a twelve-month hence. ~ *Samuel Johnson*

———— PROCRASTINATION ————

If you want to make an easy job seem mighty hard, just keep putting off doing it.

~ *Olin Miller*

Procrastination is my sin.
It brings me naught but sorrow.
I know that I should stop it.
In fact, I will—tomorrow!

~ *Gloria Pitzer*

PROGRESS

Restlessness is discontent—and discontent is the first necessity of progress. Show me a thoroughly satisfied man—and I will show you a failure.

~ *Thomas Edison*

PROMISE

When a man repeats a promise again and again he means to fail you.

If you wish to be a success in the world, promise everything, deliver nothing. ~ *Napoleon*

He who is the most slow in making a promise is the most faithful in the performance of it.

~ *Jean J. Rousseau*

One who doesn't give the gift he promised is like a cloud blowing over a desert without dropping any rain. ~ *Proverbs 25:14*

If you will promise less and do more, your boss will eventually put your name on a door.

—— PROMPTNESS ——

I am a believer in punctuality though it makes me very lonely.   ~ *E.V. Verrall*

—— PROOF ——

The proof of the pudding is in the eating.
~ *Cervantes*

—— PROPAGANDA ——

The great masses of the people will more easily fall victims to a big lie than to a small one.

~ *Adolf Hitler*

—— PROPERTY ——

Property is the fruit of labor: Property is desirable; it is a positive good.   ~ *Abraham Lincoln*

Thieves respect property. They merely wish the property to become their property that they may more perfectly respect it.   ~ *G.K. Chesterton*

―――― **PROPHESY** ――――

I always avoid prophesying beforehand, because it is much better policy to prophesy after the event has already taken place.　　～*Winston Churchill*

―――― **PROSPERITY** ――――

I'll say this for adversity: People seem to be able to stand it, and that's more than I can say for prosperity.

Few of us can stand prosperity—another man's, I mean.　　～*Mark Twain*

Prosperity discovers vice, adversity discovers virtue.　　～*Francis Bacon*

Prosperity is the surest breeder of insolence I know.

～*Mark Twain*

It requires a strong constitution to withstand repeated attacks of prosperity.

～*J.L. Basford*

If you pick up a starving dog and make him prosperous, he will not bite you; that is the principal difference between a dog and a man.

～*Mark Twain*

——— **PROSTITUTE** ———

O my son, trust my advice—stay away from prostitutes. For a prostitute is a deep and narrow grave. Like a robber, she waits for her victims as one after another become unfaithful to their wives.

~ Proverbs 23:26-28

——— **PROSTITUTION** ———

It has been said that politics is the second oldest profession. I have learned that it bears a striking resemblance to the first. *~ Ronald Reagan*

——— **PROVERB** ———

Proverbs are short sentences drawn from long experiences. *~ Cervantes*

A country can be judged by the quality of its proverbs.

——— **PSYCHIATRIST** ———

A neurotic is a man who builds a castle in the air. A psychotic is the man who lives in it. A psychiatrist is the man who collects the rent. *~ Jerome Lawrence*

Anybody who goes to see a psychiatrist ought to have his head examined. *~ Samuel Goldwyn*

A psychiatrist is a fellow who asks you a lot of expensive questions your wife asks for nothing.

~ *Joey Adams*

PSYCHOANALYSIS

Daughters go into analysis hating their fathers, and come out hating their mothers. They never come out hating themselves. ~ *Laurie Jo Wojcik*

PSYCHOTIC

The psychotic says two and two are five and the neurotic knows two and two are four, and hates it.

~ *Gordon Gammack*

PUBLICITY

What kills a skunk is the publicity it gives itself.

~ *Abraham Lincoln*

PUN

Hanging is too good for a man who makes puns; he should be drawn and quoted.

~ *Fred Allen*

A pun is the lowest form of humor—when you don't think of it first.   ~ *Oscar Levant*

——— PUNCTUAL ———

The trouble with being punctual is that nobody's there to appreciate it.   ~ *Franklin P. Jones*

There is at least one good thing you can say about punctuality—it is a sure way to help you enjoy a few minutes of complete privacy.

~ *O.A. Battista*

People who are late are often so much jollier than the people who have to wait for them.

~ *Edward V. Lucas*

——— PUNISHMENT ———

The liar's punishment is not in the least that he is not believed, but that he cannot believe anyone else.

~ *George Bernard Shaw*

——— PUZZLE ———

Nothing puzzles me more than time and space, and yet nothing puzzles me less, for I never think about them.   ~ *Charles Lamb*

——— QUARRELS ———

One of the little-mentioned but considerable advantages of rural living is that family quarrels can't be overheard. ~ *Sydney Harris*

It is hard to stop a quarrel once it starts, so don't let it begin. ~ *Proverbs 17:14*

A quarrel is quickly settled when deserted by one party; there is no battle unless there be two.

~ *Seneca*

Those who in quarrels interpose
Must often wipe a bloody nose.

~ *John Gay*

The fiercest quarrels do not always argue the greatest offences. ~ *Terence*

——— QUESTIONS ———

It is better to ask some of the questions than to know all of the answers. ~ *James Thurber*

Ask a dumb question and be embarrassed for a moment; don't ask it and be embarrassed for a lifetime.

Better ask twice than lose your way once.

~ *Danish Proverb*

It is harder to ask a sensible question than to supply a sensible answer. ~ *Persian Proverb*

My greatest strength as a consultant is to be ignorant and ask a few questions.

~ *Peter Drucker*

He who knows all the answers most likely misunderstood the questions.

——— QUOTATION ———

I often quote myself. It adds spice to my conversation. ~ *George Bernard Shaw*

Next to being witty yourself, the best thing is being able to quote another's wit. ~ *Christian N. Bovee*

The surest way to make a monkey of a man is to quote him. ~ *Robert Benchley*

Stronger than an army is a quotation whose time has come. ~ *W.I.E. Gates*

I quote others only the better to express myself.

~ *Michel de Montaigne*

By necessity, by proclivity, and by delight, we all quote. ~ *Ralph Waldo Emerson*

The wisdom of the wise and the experience of the ages are perpetuated by quotations.

~ Benjamin Disraeli

The majority of those who put together collections of verses or epigrams resemble those who eat cherries or oysters; they begin by choosing the best and end by eating everything. *~ Chamfort*

He who never quotes is never quoted.

~ Charles H. Spurgeon

——— RAGE ———

Folks who fly into a rage always make a bad landing.

——— RAPE ———

Rape is the ultimate degrading, theft, and violence that one person can do to another.

——— RASH ———

Jumping to conclusions seldom leads to happy landings.

—— READERS ——

I divide all readers into two classes: those who read to remember and those who read to forget.

~ *William Lyon Phelps*

—— READING ——

When we read too fast or too slowly, we understand nothing. ~ *Blaise Pascal*

He who doesn't read good books has no advantage over the person who cannot read them.

—— REAL ESTATE ——

Never build after you are five and forty; have five years income in hand before you lay a brick; and always calculate the expense at double the estimate.

~ *Henry Kett*

—— REALITY ——

Some wishes cannot succeed; some victories cannot be won; some loneliness is incorrigible. The only relief and freedom is in knowing what is real.

~ *Wendell Berry*

REASON

Reason is the enemy of faith.

~ *Martin Luther*

REBEL

When arguing with a rebel, don't use foolish arguments as he does, or you will become as foolish as he is! Prick his conceit with silly replies!

~ *Proverbs 26:4, 5*

REBELLION

Rebellion: The words and acts of violence by people who have been deeply hurt.

~ *R.E. Phillips*

A youngster's heart is filled with rebellion, but punishment will drive it out of him.

~ *Proverbs 22:15*

RECOLLECTION

Take notes on the spot, a note is worth a cart-load of recollections.   ~ *Ralph Waldo Emerson*

——— RECONCILIATION ———

It is much safer to reconcile an enemy than to conquer him; victory may deprive him of his poison, but reconciliation of his will.   *~ Feltham*

——— REDUCE ———

You can't reduce by talking about it. You have to keep your mouth shut.   *~ Grit*

——— REFORMERS ———

All reformers, however strict their conscience, live in houses just as big as they can pay for.

~ Logan Pearsall Smith

——— REGRET ———

Regret is an appalling waste of energy; you can't build on it; it's only good for wallowing in.

~ Katherine Mansfield

——— REJOICE ———

Why is it that we rejoice at a birth and grieve at a funeral? Is it because we are not the person concerned?   *~ Mark Twain*

Be still, sad heart, and cease repining,
Behind the clouds the sun is shining;
Thy fate is the common fate of all;
Into each life some rain must fall,
Some days must be dark and dreary.

> ~ *Henry Wadsworth
> Longfellow*

RELATIVES

Go to friends for advice,
To women for pity;
To strangers for charity;
To relatives for nothing.

> ~ *Spanish Proverb*

RELATIVITY

When a man sits with a pretty girl for an hour, it seems like a minute. But let him sit on a hot stove for a minute, and it's longer than an hour. That's relativity.

> ~ *Albert Einstein*

RELAXATION

Only when a man is at peace with himself can he find the inclination to relax.

The time to relax is when you don't have time for it.

> ~ *Sydney J. Harris*

——— RELIGION ———

Most people have some sort of religion, at least they know which church they're staying away from.

~ *John Erskine*

We have just enough religion to make us hate but not enough to make us love one another.

~ *Jonathan Swift*

If men are so wicked with religion, what would they be without it? ~ *Benjamin Franklin*

Men will wrangle for religion; write for it; fight for it; die for it; anything but live for it.

~ *Charles Colton*

——— REPARTEE ———

Repartee: What a person thinks of after he becomes a departee. ~ *Dan Bennett*

Repartee is something we think of twenty-four hours too late. ~ *Mark Twain*

Repartee: Any reply that is so clever that it makes the listener wish he had said it himself.

~ *Elbert Hubbard*

Repartee is a duel fought with the point of jokes.

~ *Max Eastman*

——— REPENT ———

As to marriage or celibacy, let a man take which course he will, he will be sure to repent.

~ Socrates

——— REPENTANCE ———

It is much easier to repent of sins that we have committed than to repent of those we intend to commit. *~ Josh Billings*

——— REPETITION ———

Repetition is the mother to talent.

——— REPORT ———

When some men discharge an obligation you can hear the report for miles around.

~ Mark Twain

——— REPRESSION ———

We have to condemn publicly the very idea that some people have the right to repress others. In keeping silent about evil, in burying it so deep within us that no sign of it appears on the surface, we are implanting it, and it will rise up a thousandfold in the future. When we neither punish or reproach evil-doers...we are ripping the foundations of justice from beneath new generations.

~ *Alexander I.*
Solzhenitsyn

——— REPUTATION ———

A reputation may be repaired, but people always keep their eyes on the place where the crack was.

If you must choose, take a good name rather than great riches; for to be held in loving esteem is better than silver and gold.   ~ *Proverbs 22:1*

Judge a man by the reputation of his enemies.

~ *Arab Proverb*

Nothing deflates so fast as a punctured reputation.

~ *Thomas Dewar*

——— RESOLUTION ———

Perhaps there is no more important component of character than steadfast resolution. The boy who is going to make a great man, or is going to count in any way in after life, must make up his mind not merely to overcome a thousand obstacles, but to win in spite of a thousand repulses and defeats.

~ *Theodore Roosevelt*

RESOURCEFULNESS

Resourcefulness is the ability to call upon creativity when needed.

RESPECT

If you steal something small you are a petty thief, but if you steal millions you are a gentleman of society.

~ Greek Proverb

RESPONSIBILITY

God is closely watching you, and he weighs carefully everything you do. *~ Proverbs 5:21*

Few things help an individual more than to place responsibility upon him, and to let him know that you trust him. *~ Booker T. Washington*

You can't escape the responsibility of tomorrow by evading it today. *~ Abraham Lincoln*

The most important thought I ever had was that of my individual responsibility to God.

~ Daniel Webster

Young man, it's wonderful to be young! Enjoy every minute of it! Do all you want to; take in everything, but realize that you must account to God for everything you do.   ~ *Ecclesiastes 11:9*

Here is my final conclusion: fear God and obey his commandments, for this is the entire duty of man. For God will judge us for everything we do, including every hidden thing, good or bad.

~ *Ecclesiastes 12:13,14*

When your shoulders are carrying a load of responsibility, there isn't room for chips.

Nothing can work me damage except myself. The harm that I sustain I carry about with me, and am never a real sufferer but by my own fault.

~ *St. Bernard*

Our main business is not to see what lies dimly at a distance, but to do what lies clearly at hand.

~ *Thomas Carlyle*

——— REST ———

A light supper, a good night's sleep, and a fine morning have often made a hero of the same man, who, by indigestion, a restless night, and a rainy morning would have proved a coward.

~ *Lord Chesterfield*

Take rest; a field that has rested gives a bountiful crop.

~ Ovid

—— RESULTS ——

The world is not interested in the storms you encountered, but whether you brought in the ship.

~ Journal of True Education

—— RETIREMENT ——

Retired is being tired twice, I've thought,
First tired of working,
Then tired of not.

~ Richard Armour

The fellow who can't figure out what to do with a Sunday afternoon is often the same one who can't wait for retirement.

The worst thing about retirement is to have to drink coffee on your own time.

When some fellers decide to retire, nobody knows the difference. *~ Kin Hubbard*

The best time to start thinking about your retirement is before the boss does.

RETORT

As surely as a wind from the north brings cold, just as surely a retort causes anger!

~ *Proverbs 25:23*

REVENGE

The best sort of revenge is not to be like him who did the injury.   ~ *Antoninus*

The only people with whom you should try to get even are those who have helped you.

~ *John E. Southard*

Revenge is often like biting a dog because the dog bit you.   ~ *Austin O'Malley*

In taking revenge a man is but equal to his enemy, but in passing over he is his superior.

~ *Francis Bacon*

REVOLUTION

The excessive increase of anything causes a reaction in the opposite direction.   ~ *Plato*

RICH

Trying to get rich quick is evil and leads to poverty.

~ *Proverbs 28:22*

The suffering of the rich is among the sweetest pleasures of the poor.   ~ *R.M. Huber*

I've been rich and I've been poor; rich is better.

~ *Sophie Tucker*

Don't knock the rich. When was the last time you were hired by somebody poor?

~ *Robert Orben*

—— RICHES ——

Many speak the truth when they say that they despise riches, but they mean the riches possessed by other men.   ~ *Charles Colton*

—— RIGHT AND WRONG ——

My specialty is being right when other people are wrong.   ~ *George Bernard Shaw*

Right is right, even if everyone is against it; and wrong is wrong, even if everyone is for it.

~ *William Penn*

Always do right. This will gratify some people and astonish the rest.   ~ *Mark Twai*

Two wrongs can never make a right.

~ *English*

——— RIGHTEOUS INDIGNATION ———

Righteous indignation: Your own wrath as opposed to the shocking bad temper of others.

~ Elbert Hubbard

——— RIGHTEOUSNESS ———

You can always tell when you are on the road of righteousness—it's uphill.   *~ Ernest Blevins*

Some folks in this world spend their whole time hunting after righteousness and can't find any time to practice it.   *~ Josh Billings*

——— ROME ———

Rome had Senators too; that's why it declined.

~ Frank Dane

It is true that Rome was not built in a day, but you haven't worked for my boss.   *~ R.E. Phillips*

——— RUIN ———

Life is short, but it is long enough to ruin any man who wants to be ruined.   *~ Josh Billings*

——— RUMOR ———

Rumor is a pipe blown by surmises, jealousies, conjectures....   ~ *William Shakespeare*

Trying to squash a rumor is like trying to unring a bell.   ~ *Shana Alexander*

——— RUT ———

Some folks will stumble through life getting out of one rut only to fall into another.

The only difference between a rut and a grave is their dimensions.   ~ *Ellen Glasgow*

He who thinks he's in the groove is often in a rut.

——— SADNESS ———

Believe me, every heart has its secret sorrows, which the world knows not; and ofttimes we call a man cold when he is only sad.   ~ *Henry Wadsworth Longfellow*

——— SAFETY ———

The desire for safety stands against every great and noble enterprise.   ~ *Tacitus*

The best safety lies in fear.

> ~ *William Shakespeare*

It is better to be safe than sorry.

> ~ *American Proverb*

——— **SAINT** ———

Living with a saint is more grueling than being one.

> ~ *Robert Neville*

The only difference between the saint and the sinner is that every saint has a past, and every sinner has a future.   ~ *Oscar Wilde*

——— **SALVATION** ———

If salvation could be attained only by working hard, then surely horses and donkeys would be in heaven.

> ~ *Martin Luther*

——— **SARCASM** ———

Sarcasm is jealousy in bold disguise.

Sarcasm comes from the Greek word "sarkasmos"

which means to rip flesh like dogs or to gnash the teeth in rage. *~R.E. Phillips*

SATIRE

The finest satire is that in which ridicule is combined with so little malice and so much conviction that it even rouses laughter in those who are hit.

~G.C. Lichtenberg

SATISFACTION

Unless each day can be looked back upon by an individual as one in which he has had some fun, some joy, some real satisfaction, that day is a loss. It is un-Christian and wicked, in my opinion, to allow such a thing to occur. *~Dwight D. Eisenhower*

There is no satisfaction in hanging a man who does not object to it. *~George Bernard Shaw*

SCANDAL

Love and scandal are the best sweeteners of tea.

~Henry Fielding

SCARE

A good scare is worth more to a man than good advice. *~Watson Edger Howe*

——— SCHIZOPHRENIC ———

Roses are red, violets are blue,
I'm a schizophrenic, and so am I.

~ Frank Crow

——— SCHOOL ———

If I ran a school, I'd give the average grade to the ones who gave me all the right answers, for being good parrots. I'd give the top grades to those who made a lot of mistakes and told me about them, and then told me what they learned from them.

~ Buckminster Fuller

I have never let my schooling interfere with my education. *~ Mark Twain*

——— SCIENCE ———

Many scientists have quit wondering how old the earth is and have begun pondering how much older it will get. *~ Grit*

I shall make electricity so cheap that only the rich can afford to burn candles. *~ Thomas Edison*

It is inexcusable for scientists to torture animals; let them make their experiments on journalists and politicians. ~ *Henrik Ibsen*

Law of Hydrodynamics: When the body is immersed in water, the telephone rings.

——— SCRATCH ———

Starting from scratch is easy; it's starting without it that's tough. ~ *Laurence Peter*

——— SEAT BELT ———

If you think a seat belt is uncomfortable, you've never tried a stretcher!

——— SECRET ———

If you would keep your secret from an enemy, tell it not to a friend. ~ *Benjamin Franklin*

He who tells a secret is another man's servant.

Three may keep a secret if two of them are dead. ~ *Benjamin Franklin*

——— SECURITY ———

Security is mortal's chiefest enemy. ~ *Ellen Terry*

Life is certainly only worthwhile as it represents struggle for worthy causes. There is no struggle in perfect security. I am quite certain that the human being could not continue to exist if he had perfect security.
 ~ *Dwight D. Eisenhower*

—— SELF ——

Looking back, my life seems like one long obstacle race, with me as its chief obstacle.
 ~ *Jack Paar*

We prefer to speak evil of ourselves rather than not speak of ourselves at all. ~ *Francois de La Rochefoucauld*

—— SELF-CENTERED ——

Edith was a little country bounded on the north, south, east, and west by Edith.
 ~ *Martha Ostenso*

—— SELF-CONFIDENCE ——

Self-confidence is the first requisite to great undertakings. ~ *Samuel Johnson*

SELF-CONTROL

It is better to be slow-tempered than famous; it is better to have self-control than to control an army.

~ *Proverbs 16:32*

SELF-DENIAL

If you begin by denying yourself nothing, the world later is apt to do your denying for you.

~ *B.F. Forbes*

SELF-DISCIPLINE

What we do upon some great occasion will probably depend on what we already are; and what we are will be the result of previous years of self-discipline.

~ *H.P. Liddon*

SELF-KNOWLEDGE

In his private heart no man much respects himself.

~ *Mark Twain*

It is not only the most difficult thing to know oneself, but the most inconvenient one, too.

~ *H.W. Shaw*

There is a great deal of unmapped country within us.

~ *George Eliot*

——— SELF-MADE ———

A self-made man? Yes—and worships his creator.

~ *William Cowper*

——— SELF-PITY ———

Sometimes I get the feeling that the whole world is against me—but deep down I know that's not true. Some of the smaller countries are neutral.

~ *Robert Orben*

——— SELF-RESPECT ———

Self-respect is the compensation you receive for respecting the rights of others.

——— SELF-SUFFICIENT ———

No man is an island, entire of itself; every man is a piece of the continent, a part of the main.

~ *John Donne*

——— SELFISHNESS ———

He who lives to benefit himself confers on the world a benefit when he dies.   ~ *Tertullian*

He that falls in love with himself will have no rivals.

~ *Benjamin Franklin*

——— SELLING ———

Everyone lives by selling something.

~ *Robert Louis Stevenson*

——— SENSITIVE ———

Some people are so sensitive they feel snubbed if an epidemic overlooks them.   ~ *Kin Hubbard*

——— SERENITY ———

God grant me the serenity
To accept the things I cannot change,
The courage to change the things I can;
And the wisdom to know the difference.

~ *Reinhold Niebur*

——— SERIOUS ———

Too much gravity argues a shallow mind.

~ *Johann Lavater*

——— SERVANT ———

The reason why rivers and seas receive the homage of a hundred mountain streams is that they keep below them. Thus they are able to reign over all the mountain streams. So the sage, wishing to be above men, putteth himself behind them. Thus, though his place be above men, they do not feel his weight; though his place be before them, they do not count it an injury.

~ Lao-Tse

——— SERVICE ———

When people are serving, life is no longer meaningless.
~ John Gardner

It is high time that the ideal of success should be replaced by the ideal of service.

~ Albert Einstein

He who sees a need and waits to be asked for help is as unkind as if he had refused it.

~ Dante

If the world is cold, make it your business to build fires.
~ Horace Traubel

If you wish to be a leader you will be frustrated, for very few people wish to be led. If you aim to be a servant you will never be frustrated.

~ Frank F. Warren

God is not greater if you reverence him, but you are greater if you serve him.   ~*Augustine*

One thing I know: the only ones among you who will be really happy are those who will have sought and found how to serve.   ~*Albert Schweitzer*

He who serves well need not fear to ask his wages.

—— SHAME ——

If a man fools me once, shame on him. If the same man fools me twice, shame on me.

~*Asian Proverb*

—— SICKNESS ——

Sickness has four stages: ill, pill, bill, will.

—— SILENCE ——

Silence is one of the hardest things to refute.

~*Josh Billings*

Silence is the wisest of replies.

~*R.E. Phillips*

There are three times when you should never say anything important to a person: when he is tired, when he is angry, and when he has just made a mistake.

A man is known by the silence he keeps.

~ *Oliver Herford*

Silence is the unbearable repartee.

~ *G.K. Chesterton*

Silence, along with modesty, is a great aid to conversation.   ~ *Michel de Montaigne*

——— SIMPLIFY ———

The ability to simplify means to eliminate the unnecessary so that the necessary may speak.

~ *Hans Hoffman*

——— SIN ———

All my life I have been seeking to climb out of the pit of my besetting sins and I cannot do it and I never will unless a hand is let down to draw me up.

~ *Seneca*

The instances are exceedingly rare of men immediately passing over a clear marked line from virtue into declared vice and corruption. There are middle tints and shades between the two extremes; there is something uncertain on the confines of the two empires which they must pass through, and which renders the change easy and imperceptible.

~ *Edmund Burke*

We are too Christian really to enjoy sinning, and too fond of sinning really to enjoy Christianity. Most of us know perfectly well what we ought to do; our trouble is that we do not want to do it.

~ *Peter Marshall*

Every sin is the result of a collaboration.

~ *Stephen Crane*

There is no sin without previous preparation.

SINCERITY

Sincerity is an openness of heart; we find it in very few people. ~ *Francois de La Rochefougauld*

SITUATIONS

It is not the situation that makes the man, but the man who makes the situation. The slave may be a freeman. The monarch may be a slave. Situations are noble or ignoble, as we make them.

~ *Frederick W. Robertson*

SKELETON

There is a skeleton in every house.

——— SKEPTICISM ———

Skepticism is a hedge against vulnerability.

~ *Charles Thomas*
Samuels

——— SLAVERY ———

Whenever I hear anyone arguing for slavery, I feel a strong impulse to see it tried on him personally.

~ *Abraham Lincoln*

——— SLEEP ———

The vigorous are no better than the lazy during one half of life, for all men are alike when asleep.

~ *Aristotle*

Sleep is the best cure for waking troubles.

~ *Cervantes*

——— SMILE ———

Smile at people. It takes seventy-two muscles to frown, only fourteen to smile.

The most powerful single thing you can do to have influence over others is to smile at them.

Most smiles are started by another smile.

~ Frank A. Clark

A smile is cheer to you and me
The cost is nothing—it's given free
It comforts the weary—gladdens the sad
Consoles those in trouble—good or bad
To rich and poor—beggar or thief
It's free to all and any belief
A natural gesture of young and old
Cheers on the faint—disarms the bold
Unlike most blessings for which we pray
It's one thing we keep when we give it away.

The smile on your face is the light in the window that tells people that you are at home.

——— SMOKING ———

To cease smoking is the easiest thing I ever did; I ought to know because I've done it a thousand times.

~ Mark Twain

Much smoking kills live men and cures dead swine.

Smoking won't send you to hell. It will just make you smell like you've been there.

~ R.E. Phillips

——— **SNAKE** ———

When you see a snake, never mind where he came from. *~W.G. Benham*

——— **SNORE** ———

People who snore always fall asleep first.

~Bits and Pieces

——— **SOBRIETY** ———

Water, taken in moderation, cannot hurt anybody.

~Mark Twain

——— **SOCIALISM** ———

The function of socialism is to raise suffering to a higher level. *~Norman Mailer*

There are two places only where socialism will work; in heaven where it is not needed, and in hell where they already have it. *~Winston Churchill*

——— **SOCIETY** ———

Society rests upon conscience and not upon science. *~Henri-Frederic Amiel*

——— SOLITUDE ———

Solitude: A good place to visit, but a poor place to stay.　　　　　　　*~ Josh Billings*

The best thinking has been done in solitude. The worst has been done in turmoil.

~ Thomas Edison

——— SOLUTION ———

A problem well-stated is a problem half-solved.

~ Charles F. Kettering

——— SORROW ———

There is a sweet joy which comes to us through sorrow.　　　　　　*~ Charles H. Spurgeon*

Every heart hath its own ache.

~ Thomas Fuller

Sorrow is like a precious treasure, shown only to friends.　　　　　　*~ African Proverb*

Never allow your own sorrow to absorb you, but seek out another to console, and you will find consolation.　　　　　　*~ J.C. Macaulay*

There can be no rainbow without a cloud and a storm.
~*J.H. Vincent*

—— SOUND ——

The empty vessel makes the greatest sound.
~*William Shakespeare*

—— SPECULATE ——

There are two times in a man's life when he should not speculate: when he can't afford it, and when he can.
~*Mark Twain*

—— SPEECH ——

When at a loss how to go on, cough.
~*Greek Proverb*

A closed mouth gathers no feet.
~*American Proverb*

A closed mouth catches no flies.
~*French Proverb*

If you haven't struck oil in your first three minutes, stop boring!
~*George Jessel*

More have repented of speech than silence.

Three things matter in a speech: who says it, how he says it, and what he says... and, of the three, the last matters the least.   *~ Lord Morley*

Criminologists claim few acts of violence are committed after a hearty meal. This prolongs the life of speakers.

The more you say, the less people remember.
    ~ Anatole France

Many people who have the gift of gab don't know how to wrap it up.   *~ Lions Magazine*

The difference between a successful career and a mediocre one sometimes consists of leaving about four or five things a day unsaid.

Two great talkers will not travel far together.
    ~ Spanish Proverb

He who says nothing shows a fine command of the language.

It usually takes me more than three weeks to prepare a good impromptu speech.
    ~ Mark Twain

Words in haste do friendships waste.

Speech is the index of the mind.

~ *Seneca*

I disapprove of what you say, but I will defend to the death your right to say it.　~ *Voltaire*

—— SPORT ——

The trouble with being a good sport is that you have to lose to prove it.　~ *Bits and Pieces*

Sports like baseball, football, basketball, and hockey develop muscles. That's why Americans have the strongest eyes in the world.　~ *Robert Orben*

Sports do not build character. They reveal it.

~ *Heywood Broun*

—— SPOUSE ——

If you fear you are losing your spouse and wonder why, make a record of your conversation with him or her and then play it back to yourself.

—— STANDSTILL ——

The rush hour traffic is at a standstill.

___

STATISTIC

A single death is a tragedy, a million deaths is a statistic. *~Joseph Stalin*

STEALING

He who steals a pin will steal a greater thing.

STORY

Don't tell a good story even though you know one; its narration will simply remind your hearers of a bad one. *~Edgar Watson Howe*

STRENGTH

One, on God's side, is a majority.

~Wendell Phillips

STRIFE

It is an honor for a man to stay out of a fight. Only fools insist on quarreling. *~Proverbs 20:3*

STRUGGLE

We are not at our best perched at the summit; we

are climbers, at our best when the way is steep.

~ *John W. Gardner*

------ **STUBBORNNESS** ------

Mules and human jackasses are proverbially stubborn.
~ *T.C. Haliburton*

------ **STUDY** ------

As turning the logs will make a dull fire burn, so change of studies a dull brain.

~ *Henry Wadsworth Longfellow*

------ **STUPIDITY** ------

He was born stupid and greatly improved his birthright.
~ *Samuel Butler*

Ordinarily he is insane. But he has lucid moments when he is only stupid.
~ *Heinrich Heine*

------ **SUCCESS** ------

Success is the one unpardonable sin against one's fellows.
~ *Ambrose Bierce*

Success has made failures of many men.

Success is simply a matter of luck. Ask any failure.

~ *Earl Wilson*

Nothing recedes like success.

Eighty percent of success is showing up.

~ *Woody Allen*

Success consists of getting up just one more time than you fall.   ~ *Oliver Goldsmith*

If you want to know how long it will take to get to the top, consult a calendar. If you want to know how long it takes to fall to the bottom, try a stopwatch.

All you need in life is ignorance and confidence, and then success is assured.   ~ *Mark Twain*

It takes about twenty years to become an overnight success.   ~ *Eddie Cantor*

Success covers a multitude of blunders.

~ *George Bernard Shaw*

This is the foundation of success nine times out of ten—having confidence in yourself and applying yourself with all your might to your work.

~ *Thomas E. Wils*

Anyone can sympathize with the sufferings of a friend, but it requires a very fine nature to sympathize with a friend's success.   ~*Oscar Wilde*

The door to the room of success swings on the hinges of opposition.

Success sits throned beyond two swinging doors marked "Push" and "Pull."

He who itches for success must be willing to scratch for it.

——— SUCKER ———

There's a sucker born every minute.

~*P.T. Barnum*

Every crowd has a silver lining.

~*P.T. Barnum*

——— SUFFERING ———

Out of suffering have emerged the strongest souls; the most massive characters are sheared with scars.

~*E.H. Chapin*

You must submit to supreme suffering in order to discover the completion of joy.

~*John Calvin*

No pain, no palm; no thorns, no throne; no gall, no glory; no cross, no crown. ~ *William Penn*

No pain, no gain.

—— **SUGGESTIONS** ——

Friendly suggestions are as pleasant as perfume.
~ *Proverbs 27:9*

—— **SUICIDE** ——

Suicide sometimes proceeds from cowardice, but not always; for cowardice sometimes prevents it, since as many live because they are afraid to die as die because they are afraid to live.

~ *Charles Colton*

Suicide is one hundred and eighty degree murder. A person has to be mad enough to kill. To kill themselves. ~ *R.E. Phillips*

—— **SUN** ——

Make hay while the sun shines.
~ *Cervantes*

——— SUNRISE ———

If God wanted us to enjoy sunrises, He would have made them come at ten o'clock in the morning.

~*Jim Slevcove*

——— SUNSHINE ———

Those who bring sunshine into the lives of others cannot keep it from themselves.

~*James M. Barrie*

——— SUPERSTITION ———

Superstition is the only religion of which base souls are capable.   ~*Joseph Joubert*

——— SUSPICION ———

Most of our suspicions of others are aroused by our knowledge of ourselves.

——— SWEARING ———

Profane swearing never did any man any good. No man is the richer or wiser or happier for it.

~*Louth*

—— SYMPATHY ——

No one really understands the grief or joy of another. *~ Franz Schubert*

In all matters of opinion, our adversaries are insane.

~ Mark Twain

—— TACT ——

Tact: Ability to tell a man he's open-minded when he has a hole in his head. *~ F.G. Kernan*

Do not use a hatchet to remove a fly from your friend's forehead. *~ Chinese Proverb*

Tact is like a girdle. It enables you to organize the awkward truth more attractively.

Tact is the ability to describe others as they see themselves. *~ Abraham Lincoln*

A spoonful of honey will catch more flies than a gallon of vinegar. *~ Benjamin Franklin*

Tact is the art of making a point without making an enemy.

—— TALK ——

Don't talk so much. You keep putting your foot in your mouth. Be sensible and turn off the flow!

~ Proverbs 10:19

Those who love to talk will suffer the consequences. Men have died for saying the wrong thing!

~ *Proverbs 18:21*

After all is said and done, more is said than done.

As empty vessels make the loudest sound, so they that have the least wit are the greatest babblers.

~ *Plato*

Don't be afraid to talk to yourself. It's the only way you can be sure somebody's listening.

~ *Franklin P. Jones*

It is all right if you talk to yourself. It is all right if you answer yourself. But when you start disagreeing with the answers, you've got a problem.

~ *R.E. Phillips*

Wise men talk because they have something to say; fools, because they have to say something.

~ *Plato*

Talk to a man about himself and he will listen for hours.　　~ *Benjamin Disraeli*

Great boaster, little doer.

Better to let them wonder why you didn't talk than why you did.

The secret of being tiresome is in telling everything.
~ Voltaire

TAX COLLECTOR

What is the difference between a taxidermist and a tax collector? The taxidermist takes only your skin.

~ Mark Twain

TAXES

Death and taxes may be the only certainties in life, but nowhere is it written that we have to tax ourselves to death.
~ Nation's Business

It seems a little ridiculous now, but this country was originally founded as a protest against taxation.

Taxation without representation is tyranny.

~ James Otis

Taxation with representation ain't so hot either.

~ Gerald Barzan

No matter how bad a child is, he is still good for a tax deduction.
~ American Proverb

Milk the cow but do not pull off the udder.

~ Greek Proverb

I'm proud to be paying taxes in the United States. The only thing is, I could be just as proud for half the money. ~ *Arthur Godfrey*

The income tax has made more liars out of American people than golf has. ~ *Will Rogers*

Those who complain about taxes can be divided into two classes: men and women.

It has reached a point where taxes are a form of capital punishment.

—— **TEACHER** ——

A teacher affects eternity; no one can tell where his influence stops. ~ *Henry Adams*

I had, out of my sixty teachers, a scant half dozen who couldn't have been supplanted by phonographs.
~ *Don Herold*

To teach is to learn. ~ *Japanese Proverb*

I hear and I forget. I see and I remember. I do and I understand. ~ *Chinese Proverb*

To teach is to learn twice.
~ *Joseph Joubert*

A teacher who is attempting to teach without inspiring the pupil with a desire to learn is hammering on cold iron. ~ *Horace Mann*

—— TEAM SPIRIT ——

If anything goes bad, I did it.
If anything goes semi-good, then we did it.
If anything goes real good, then you did it.

~ *Bear Bryant*

—— TEAR ——

Kiss the tear from her lip,
You'll find the rose
The sweeter for the dew.

~ *Webster*

—— TEARS ——

More tears are shed in our theaters over fancied tragedies than in our churches over real ones.

~ *Frank C. Rideout*

—— TEENAGER ——

Nobody can be so amusingly arrogant as a young man who has just discovered an old idea and thinks it is his own.   ~ *Sydney Harris*

Sometimes a young person is bad because he hates to waste a reputation. ~ *John K. Young*

There's nothing wrong with teenagers that reasoning with them won't aggravate.

To get his teenage son to clean his room one father just throws the keys to the family car in there once a week. ~ *Lane Olinghouse*

It is amazing how quickly the kids learn to drive a car, yet are unable to understand the lawnmower, snowblower, or vacuum cleaner.

~ *Ben Bergor*

Good advice to parents whose teenagers are learning to drive: Don't stand in their way!

—— TELEVISION ——

Television has changed the American child from an irresistible force into an immovable object.

Television requires nothing of us, but in requiring nothing, takes the most valuable possession we have: our time. ~ *Nuggets*

I find television very educating. Every time somebody turns on the set I go into the other room and read a book. ~ *Groucho Marx*

Pure drivel tends to drive ordinary drivel off the TV screen. ~ *Marvin Kitman*

The easiest way to find more time to do all the things you want to do is to turn off the television.

~ *O.A. Battista*

——— TEMPER ———

When you are right, you can afford to keep your temper; when you are wrong, you can't afford to lose it.

——— TEMPTATION ———

What makes resisting temptation difficult, for many people, is that they don't want to discourage it completely.   ~ *Franklin P. Jones*

Satan is not such a fool as to fish without bait.

No one knows how bad he is until he has tried to be good. There is a silly idea about that good people don't know what temptation means.

~ *C.S. Lewis*

If God bolts the door, do not get through the window.

No one can be caught in places he does not visit.

If you don't touch the rope, you won't ring the bell.

When fleeing temptation, don't leave a forwarding address. ~*R.E. Phillips*

The forces of temptation often attack a man's garrison of resolution by surprise, to win a quick victory and blow up the walls of fortification.

~*Douglas Meador*

Temptations, unlike opportunities, will always give you a second chance. ~*O.A. Battista*

Opportunity knocks only once; temptation leans on the doorbell.

TEN COMMANDMENTS

The Supreme Court has handed down the eleventh commandment: "Thou shalt not, in thy classrooms, read the first ten." ~*Fletcher Knebel*

TERROR

The one means that wins the easiest victory over reason: terror and force. ~*Adolf Hitler*

TERRORIZE

No one can terrorize a whole nation unless we are all his accomplices. ~*Edward R. Murrow*

——— THANKFULNESS ———

If you can't be satisfied with what you have received, be thankful for what you have escaped.

If a fellow isn't thankful for what he's got, he isn't likely to be thankful for what he's going to get.

~Frank A. Clark

There's one thing for which you can be thankful— only you and God have all the facts about yourself.

~Dub Nance

——— THEORIES ———

Before I got married I had six theories about bringing up children; now I have six children, and no theories.   *~Lord Rochester*

——— THINK ———

If I look confused, it's because I'm thinking.

~Sam Goldwyn

If everybody thought before they spoke, the silence would be deafening.   *~Gerald Barzan*

——— THINKING ———

There are two ways to slide easily through life: to believe everything or to doubt everything; both ways save us from thinking.   *~ Alfred Korzybski*

There is no expedient to which a man will not go to avoid the real labor of thinking.

~ Thomas Edison

Thinking is when your mouth stays shut and your head keeps talking to itself.

Thinking is the hardest work there is, which is probably why so few engage in it.

~ Henry Ford

The probable reason some people get lost in thought is because it is unfamiliar territory to them.

——— THOROUGHNESS ———

The heart of the prudent acquires knowledge, and the ear of the wise seeks knowledge.

~ Proverbs 18:15 (NKJV)

——— THOUGHT ———

Life does not consist mainly—or even largely—of facts and happenings. It consists mainly of the storm of thoughts that is forever blowing through one's head.

~ *Mark Twain*

Men can live without air for a few minutes, without water for about two weeks, without food for about two months—and without a new thought for years on end.

~ *Kent Ruth*

Everything has been thought of before, but the problem is to think of it again.

—— **THRIFT** ——

Take care of your pennies and your dollars will take care of themselves. ~ *Scottish Proverb*

—— **TIME** ——

Our greatest danger in life is in permitting the urgent things to crowd out the important.

~ *Charles E. Hummel*

Time is a great healer, but a poor beautician.

~ *Lucille S. Harper*

Dost thou love life? Then do not squander time, for that is the stuff life is made of.

~ *Benjamin Franklin*

Time and tide wait for no man.

~ *Geoffrey Chaucer*

Time and tide wait for no man, but time always stands still for a woman of thirty.

~ *Robert Frost*

It is later than you think. ~ *Chinese Proverb*

Lost, yesterday, somewhere between sunrise and sunset, two golden hours, each set with sixty diamond minutes. No reward is offered, for they are gone forever.

~ *Horace Mann*

Take all the swift advantage of the hours.

~ *William Shakespeare*

The person who always watches the clock will never become the man of the hour.

We never shall have any more time. We have, and we have always had, all the time there is.

~ *Arnold Bennett*

Since thou art not sure of a minute, throw not away an hour.

~ *Benjamin Franklin*

Time cures sorrows and squabbles because we all change, and are no longer the same persons. Neither the offender nor the offended is the same.

~ *Blaise Pascal*

A stitch in time saves nine.

~ *English Proverb*

Time flies. It's up to you to be the navigator.
> ~ *Robert Orben*

——— TODAY ———

One today is worth two tomorrows.
> ~ *Benjamin Franklin*

——— TOLERANT ———

Nothing makes you more tolerant of a neighbor's noisy party than being there.

——— TOMBSTONE ———

The tombstone is about the only thing that can stand upright and lie on its face at the same time.
> ~ *Mary Wilson Little*

——— TOMORROW ———

Never put off till tomorrow what you can do the day after tomorrow. ~ *Mark Twain*

Tomorrow is the most important thing in life. It comes into us at midnight very clean. It's perfect when it arrives and it puts itself in our hands. It hopes we've learned something from yesterday.

~ *John Wayne*

Never put off till tomorrow what you can do today.

~ *Lord Chesterfield*

Do it tomorrow. You've made enough mistakes for one day.   ~ Bumper Sticker

——— TONGUE ———

A slip of the foot may be soon recovered, but that of the tongue perhaps never.

Learn to hold thy tongue. Five words cost Zacharias forty weeks' silence.   ~ *Fuller*

A tart temper never mellows with age, and a sharp tongue is the only edged tool that grows keener with constant use.   ~ *Washington Irving*

A tongue doesn't weigh much, but many people have trouble holding one.   ~ *Grit*

He missed an invaluable opportunity to hold his tongue.   ~ *Andrew Lang*

Teach your child to hold his tongue; he'll learn fast enough to speak.   ~ *Benjamin Franklin*

A tattler is worse than a thief.

How oftentimes is silence the wisest of replies.

The tongue is not steel—yet it cuts.

He knows much who knows how to hold his tongue.

Many have fallen by the edge of the sword, but more have fallen by the tongue.

The tongue is in a wet place and slips easily.

> ~*R.E. Phillips*

More have repented of speech than silence.

We ought either to be silent or to speak things that are better than silence.

One man may teach another to speak; but none can teach another to hold his peace.

No echoes return to mock the silent tongue.

—— TRAGEDY ——

In the theater there is comedy and tragedy. If the house is packed it's a comedy, otherwise it's a tragedy.

> ~*Sol Hurok*

In this world there are only two tragedies: one is not getting what one wants, and the other is getting it.

~ *Oscar Wilde*

Tragedy warms the soul, elevates the heart, can and ought to create heroes.   ~ *Napoleon*

—————— **TRANSGRESSOR** ——————

The reason the way of the transgressor is hard is because it's so crowded.   ~ *Frank Hubbard*

—————— **TRIALS** ——————

The diamond cannot be polished without friction, nor man perfected without trials.

Trying times are times for trying.

All sunshine makes a desert.

—————— **TRIFLE** ——————

Events of great consequence often spring from trifling circumstances.   ~ *Livy*

—————— **TROUBLE** ——————

When I dig another out of trouble, the hole from which I lift him is the place where I bury my own.

I am an old man and have known a great many troubles, but most of them never happened.

~ Mark Twain

We should never attempt to bear more than one kind of trouble at once. Some people bear three kinds—all they have had, all they have now, and all they expect to have. *~ Edward Everett Hale*

Troubles, like babies, grow larger by nursing.

~ Lady Holland

It always looks darkest just before it gets totally black. *~ Charlie Brown*

No one is more exasperating than the guy who can always see the bright side of our misfortunes.

If you see ten troubles coming down the road, you can be sure that nine will run into the ditch before they reach you. *~ Calvin Coolidge*

The gem cannot be polished without friction, nor men perfected without trials.

~ Chinese Proverb

Warning! Following are the names of the seven Mischievous Misses who are responsible for most of our troubles: Miss Information, Miss Quotation, Miss Representation, Miss Interpretation, Miss Construction, Miss Conception, Miss Understanding. Don't listen to them. *~ William J.H. Boetcker*

As long as you laugh at your troubles, you may be sure that you will never run out of something to laugh at.

Jesus spoke more about trouble and crosses and persecution than he did about human happiness.

~ *W.T. Purkiser*

For every ailment under the sun,
There is a remedy, or there is none;
If there be one, try to find it;
If there be none, never mind it.

~ *Mother Goose*

There is nothing so consoling as to find that one's neighbor's troubles are at least as great as one's own.

~ *Charles de Montesquieu*

——— TRUST ———

If you want favor with both God and man, and a reputation for good judgment and common sense, then trust the Lord completely; don't ever trust yourself. In everything you do, put God first, and he will direct you and crown your efforts with success.

~ *Proverbs 3:5, 6*

Trust, like fine china, once broken can be repaired but it is never quite the same.

~ *Chinese Proverb*

A mighty fortress is our God,
A bulwark never failing,
Our helper he amid the flood
Of mortal ills prevailing.

~ Martin Luther

I told God that I had done all that I could and that now the result was in his hands; that if this country was to be saved, it was because he so willed it! The burden rolled off my shoulders. My intense anxiety was relieved and in its place came a great trustfulness!

~ Abraham Lincoln

——— TRUTH ———

Why shouldn't truth be stranger than fiction? Fiction, after all, has to make sense.

~ Mark Twain

Fraud and falsehood only dread examination. Truth invites it.   *~ Thomas Cooper*

The best way to show that a stick is crooked is not to argue about it or to spend time denouncing it, but to lay a straight stick alongside it.

~ D.L. Moody

The truth shall make you free, but first it shall make you miserable.   *~ Barry Stevens*

Truth has to change hands only a few times to become fiction.

Truth is always strong, no matter how weak it looks, and falsehood is always weak, no matter how strong it looks. *~ Phillips Brooks*

Men occasionally stumble over the truth, but most of them pick themselves up and hurry off as if nothing had happened. *~ Winston Churchill*

Just why do men lie about each other when the plain truth would be bad enough?

When in doubt, tell the truth.

~ Mark Twain

If you tell the truth, you don't have to remember anything. *~ Mark Twain*

And ye shall know the truth, and the truth shall make you free. *~ John 8:32* (KJV)

Truth is incontrovertible. Panic may resent it; ignorance may deride it; malice may distort it; but there it is. *~ Winston Churchill*

Pretty much all the honest truth-telling there is in the world is done by children.

~ Oliver Wendell Holmes

——— **TYRANNY** ———

He who strikes terror into others is himself in continual fear. *~ Claudian*

—— UNCERTAINTY ——

We live in the midst of alarms; anxiety beclouds the future; we expect some new disaster with each newspaper we read. *~ Abraham Lincoln*

In times like these, it helps to recall that there have always been times like these. *~ Paul Harvey*

—— UNDERSTANDING ——

A simple rule in dealing with those who are hard to get along with is to remember that this person is striving to assert his superiority; and you must deal with him from that point of view. *~ Alfred Adler*

—— UNHAPPINESS ——

The most unhappy of all men is he who believes himself to be so. *~ David Hume*

A person is never as happy or as unhappy as he thinks he is. *~ Francois*
de La Rochefoucauld

—— UNRELIABLE ——

Putting confidence in an unreliable man is like chewing with a sore tooth, or trying to run on a broken foot. *~ Proverbs 25:19*

——— UNSELFISHNESS ———

The secret of being loved is in being lovely; and the secret of being lovely is in being unselfish.

~ *J.G. Holland*

The wise man does not lay up treasure. The more he gives to others, the more he has for his own.

~ *Lao-Tse*

Grief and pain are but the soil from which springs the lovely plant—unselfishness. Be gentle and learn how to suffer.... Whatever you can do to live bravely— without impatience or repining—will help you to live some day in joyful contentment.

~ *Helen Keller*

——— VACATION ———

A day away from some people is like a month in the country.   ~ *Howard Dietz*

No one needs a vacation so much as the person who has just had one.   ~ *Elbert Hubbard*

——— VACUUM ———

There is a God-shaped vacuum in every heart, and man is restless until it is filled by him.

~ *Blaise Pascal*

VALOR

The better part of valor is discretion.

~ *William Shakespeare*

Brave deeds are wasted when hidden.

~ *Blaise Pascal*

VALUES

The world has forgotten, in its concern with Left and Right, that there is an Above and Below.

~ *Glen Drake*

VANITY

Vanity is often the unseen spur.

~ *William M. Thackeray*

Some people are so intractably vain that when they admit they are wrong they want as much credit for admitting it as if they were right.

~ *Sydney Harris*

VARIETY

Variety's the very spice of life, that gives it all its flavor. ~ *William Cowper*

——— VICE ———

It has been my experience that folks who have no vices have very few virtues. ~*Abraham Lincoln*

——— VICE PRESIDENT ———

Once there were two brothers: one ran away to sea, the other was elected vice president—and nothing was ever heard from either of them again.

~ *Thomas Marshall*

A vice president is a person who finds a molehill on his desk in the morning and must make a mountain out of it by five P.M. ~*Fred Allen*

The man with the best job in the country is the vice president. All he has to do is get up every morning and say, "How's the president?" ~*Will Rogers*

——— VICTORY ———

Victory goes to the player who makes the next-to-the-last mistake.

Victory is gained only through conflict.

One of the greatest victories you can gain over a man is to beat him at politeness.

~ *Bits and Pieces*

VILLAIN

One may smile, and smile, and be a villain.

~ *William Shakespeare*

VIRTUE

Virtue is to herself the best reward.

~ *Henry Moore*

VISIT

Visits always give pleasure—if not the coming, then the going.

VOLUME

Every man is a volume, if you know how to read him.

~ *Channing*

VOTE

Whenever a fellow tells me he's bipartisan, I know he's going to vote against me.

~ *Harry S. Truman*

—— WAGES ——

The laborer is worthy of his hire.

> ~ *Luke 10:7* (KJV)

—— WAITING ——

While we keep a man waiting, he reflects on our shortcomings. ~ *French Proverb*

All things come to him who waits—even justice.

> ~ *Austin O'Malley*

—— WAR ——

I don't know what kind of weapons will be used in the third world war, assuming there will be a third world war. But I can tell you what the fourth world war will be fought with—stone clubs.

> ~ *Albert Einstein*

Human war has been the most successful of all our cultural traditions. ~ *Robert Ardrey*

Grass never grows where my horse has trod.

> ~ *Attila the Hun*

In the last 3,421 years of recorded history only 268 have seen no war. ~ *Will and Ariel Durant*

—— WASTE ——

Waste not, want not.

—— WATERMELON ——

When one has tasted it [watermelon] he knows what the angels eat. ~ *Mark Twain*

—— WEALTH ——

Discipline begets abundance. Abundance, unless we use the utmost care, destroys discipline.

Don't weary yourself trying to get rich. Why waste your time? For riches can disappear as though they had the wings of a bird! ~ *Proverbs 23:4, 5*

After a rich man gets rich, his next ambition is to get richer. ~ *American Proverb*

God shows his contempt for wealth by the kind of person he selects to receive it.

~ *Austin O'Malley*

—— WEATHER ——

Don't knock the weather; nine tenths of the people couldn't start a conversation if it didn't change once in a while. ~ *Kin Hubbard*

Everybody talks about the weather but nobody does anything about it.   *~ Mark Twain*

—— **WEIGHT** ——

All you have to do to lose weight is mix plenty of self-control with everything you eat.

—— **WELCOME** ——

Don't visit your neighbor too often, or you will outwear your welcome!   *~ Proverbs 25:17*

—— **WHALE** ——

It isn't so hard to believe a whale swallowed Jonah considering what some fellows feed their girlfriends, who swallow it in a single gulp.

—— **WHO** ——

I keep six honest serving men
(They taught me all I knew);
Their names are What and Why and When
And How and Where and Who.

          ~ Rudyard Kipling

——— WICKED ———

No man ever becomes wicked all at once.

~ *Bits and Pieces*

——— WIFE ———

A worthy wife is her husband's joy and crown; the other kind corrodes his strength and tears down everything he does. ~ *Proverbs 12:4*

The man who finds a wife finds a good thing; she is a blessing to him from the Lord.

~ *Proverbs 18:22*

A cheerful wife is the joy of life.

Whether you wind up with a nest egg or a goose egg depends on the kind of chick you married.

~ *Wall Street Journal*

The man who says his wife can't take a joke forgets that she took him.

The weeping bride makes a laughing wife.

——— WILL ———

Put your will in neutral so God can shift you.

Where there's a will, there's a way.

~ English Proverb

——— WILLING ———

The world is full of willing people; some willing to work, the rest willing to let them.

~ Robert Frost

——— WIN ———

It isn't whether you win or lose. It's how you place the blame.

If you cannot win, make the one ahead of you break the record. *~ Jan McKeithen*

——— WINE ———

Don't let the sparkle and smooth taste of strong wine deceive you. For in the end it bites like a poisonous serpent; it stings like an adder.

~ Proverbs 23:31, 32

——— WISDOM ———

How does a man become wise? The first step is to trust and reverence the Lord!

~ Proverbs 1:7-9

A man begins cutting his wisdom teeth the first time he bites off more than he can chew.

~ Herb Caen

Never thumb your nose at a man on a rock pile.

Committing a great truth to memory is admirable; committing it to life is wisdom.

~ William A. Ward

Wise men learn more from fools than fools from wise men. *~ Cato*

A wise man sees as much as he ought, not as much as he can. *~ Michel de Montaigne*

The older I grow, the more I distrust the familiar doctrine that age brings wisdom.

~ H.L. Mencken

Wise men are not always silent, but know when to be.

The fear of the Lord is the beginning of wisdom.

~ Psalm 11:10 (KJV)

———— **WISE** ————

The art of being wise is the art of knowing what to overlook. *~ William James*

He is a wise man who does not grieve for the things which he has not, but rejoices for those which he has.

~ Epictetus

WISHBONE

A man will sometimes devote all his life to the development of one part of his body—the wishbone.

~ Robert Frost

WISHES

It is not good for all your wishes to be fulfilled. Through sickness you recognize the value of health, through evil the value of good, through hunger satisfaction, through exertion the value of rest.

~ Heraclitus

WISHING

Wishes never filled the bag.

With wishing comes grieving.

What ardently we wish we soon believe.

~ Edward Young

Our blunders mostly come from letting our wishes interpret our duties.   *~ A. Maclaren*

—— WIT ——

After wisdom comes wit. *~Evan Esar*

Wit is the salt of conversation, not the food.
~William Hazlitt

Brevity is the soul of wit. *~William Shakespeare*

The greatest advantage I know of being thought a wit by the world is that it gives one the greater freedom of playing the fool. *~Jonathan Swift*

Wit in conversation is, in the midwives' phrase, a quick conception and an easy delivery.
~Jonathan Swift

Wit is the sudden marriage of ideas which before their marriage were not perceived to have any relationship. *~Mark Twain*

—— WOMAN ——

A woman can make a man feel older or younger than his years if she so chooses.

Even if you understood women—you'd never believe it. *~Frank Dane*

There are two ways to handle a woman, and nobody knows either of them. *~Kin Hubbard*

It is not true that woman was made from man's rib; she was really made from his funny bone.

~ *Ames Barrie*

Being a woman is a terribly difficult task since it consists principally in dealing with men.

Women were made with a sense of humor so they could love men instead of laughing at them.

~ *Will Rogers*

When a woman is speaking to you, listen to what she says with her eyes. ~ *Victor Hugo*

Women are never stronger than when they arm themselves with their weakness.

~ *Marquise du Deffand*

Most men who run down women are running down one woman only. ~ *Remy de Gourmont*

—— WOMEN'S RIGHTS ——

Yesterday I was at a wedding where the minister looked at the couple and solemnly pronounced them person and person. ~ *Robert Orben*

Men now monopolize the upper levels...depriving women of their rightful share of opportunities for incompetence. ~ *Laurence Peter*

WORD

The difference between the right word and the almost right word is the difference between lightning and the lightning bug.　　*~ Mark Twain*

A word fitly spoken is like apples of gold in pictures of silver.　　*~ Proverbs 25:11* (KJV)

WORDS

Kind words are like honey—enjoyable and healthful.　　*~ Proverbs 16:24*

The man of few words and settled mind is wise; therefore, even a fool is thought to be wise when he is silent. It pays him to keep his mouth shut.

~ Proverbs 17:27, 28

Language is the dress of thought.

~ Samuel Johnson

Words are things; and a small drop of ink,
Falling like dew upon a thought, produces
That which makes thousands, perhaps millions,
　　think.

~ Lord Byron

Four-letter words that changed the world: love, hope, care, heal, work, feel, duty, home, good, kind, pity, rest, seek, pray, live.

He who speaks much is much mistaken.

—— WORK ——

To get the true measure of a man's capacity, note how much more he does than is required of him.

There never has been any thirty-hour week for men who had anything to do.   ~ *Charles F. Kettering*

Anyone can do any amount of work provided it isn't the work he is supposed to be doing at that moment.

~ *Robert Benchley*

I've met a few people in my time who were enthusiastic about hard work. And it was just my luck that all of them happened to be men I was working for at the time.   ~ *Bill Gold*

The average human being in any line of work could double his productive capacity overnight if he began right now to do all the things he knows he should do, and to stop doing all the things he knows he should not do.   ~ *Elmer G. Letterman*

Few men ever drop dead from overwork, but many quietly curl up and die because of undersatisfaction.

~ *Sydney Harris*

Unless a man has to do more than he can do, he will not do all that he can do.   ~ *Henry Drummond*

Would you like to find out what it's like to be a member of a minority group? Try putting in an honest day's work occasionally. ~ *Kelly Fordyce*

For a real quick energy boost, nothing beats having the boss walk in. ~ *Robert Orben*

The hardest thing about making a living is that you have to do it again the next day.

~ *Quote*

A man grows most tired while standing still.

~ *Chinese Proverb*

I never remember feeling tired by work, though idleness exhausts me completely.

~ *Sherlock Holmes*

Work expands so as to fill the time available for its completion. ~ *Parkinson's Law*

I never did a day's work in my life. It was all fun.

~ *Thomas Edison*

I know hardly anyone who works too hard. I believe in hard work and long hours of work. Men do not break down from overwork, but from worry and from plunging into dissipation and efforts not aligned with their work. ~ *Charles Evans Hughes*

Work is the true elixir of life. The busiest man is the happiest man. Excellence in any art or profession is attained only by hard and persistent work.

~ *Sir Theodore Martin*

Happiness, I have discovered, is nearly always a rebound from hard work. It is one of the follies of men to imagine that they can enjoy mere thought, or emotion, or sentiment. As well try to eat beauty! For happiness must be tricked! She loves to see men at work. She loves sweat, weariness, self-sacrifice.

~ David Grayson

Thank God every morning when you get up that you have something to do which must be done, whether you like it or not. Being forced to work, and forced to do your best, will breed in you temperance, self-control, diligence, strength of will, content, and a hundred other virtues which the idle never know.

~ Charles Kingsley

No, work is not an ethical duty imposed upon us from without by a misguided and outmoded Puritan morality; it is a manifestation of man's deepest desire that the days of his life shall have significance.

~ Harold W. Dodds

My father taught me to work; he did not teach me to love it. *~ Abraham Lincoln*

There is a wonderful power in honest work to develop latent energies and reveal a man to himself.

I do most of my work sitting down; that's where I shine. *~ Robert Benchley*

Every man's work is a portrait of himself.

All work and no play makes Jack a dull boy.

~ James Howell

——— WORMS ———

All modern men are descended from wormlike creatures, but it shows more on some people.

~ Will Cuppy

——— WORRY ———

Worry is a thin stream of fear trickling through the mind. If encouraged, it cuts a channel into which all other thoughts are drained. *~ A.S. Roche*

The soil of tension and frenzy is productive of the plant of worry. *~ John Haggai*

Worry often gives a small thing a big shadow.

~ Peb Jackson

We would worry less about what others think of us if we realized how seldom they do.

~ Ethel Barrett

How much have cost us the evils that never happened! *~ Thomas Jefferson*

Worry is faith in the negative, trust in the unpleasant, assurance of disaster, and belief in defeat.... Worry is a magnet that attracts negative conditions; faith is a more powerful force that creates positive circumstances.... Worry is wasting today's time to clutter up tomorrow's opportunities with yesterday's troubles. ~ *William A. Ward*

Worry is interest paid on trouble before it falls due.

~ *William Ralph Inge*

Take therefore no thought for the morrow; for the morrow shall take thought for the things of itself. Sufficient unto the day is the evil thereof.

~ *Matthew 6:34 KJV*

Do you remember the things you were worrying about a year ago? How did they work out? Didn't you waste a lot of fruitless energy on account of most of them? Didn't most of them turn out all right after all?

~ *Dale Carnegie*

Don't cross your bridges until you come to them.

Don't cry over spilt milk.

If you can't sleep, then get up and do something instead of lying there and worrying. It's the worry that gets you, not the loss of sleep.

~ *Dale Carnegie*

To conquer fear and worry, keep busy!

> ~ *Dale Carnegie*

By forgetting the past and by throwing myself into other interests, I forget to worry.

> ~ *Jack Dempsey*

Happy is the man who has broken the chains which hurt the mind, and has given up worrying once and for all. ~ *Ovid*

Early in my business career I learned the folly of worrying about anything. I have always worked as hard as I could, but when a thing went wrong and could not be righted, I dismissed it from my mind.

> ~ *Julius Rosenwald*

It is the little bits of things that fret and worry us; we can dodge an elephant, but we can't a fly.

> ~ *Josh Billings*

It is not work that kills men; it is worry. Work is healthy; you can hardly put more upon a man than he can bear. Worry is rust upon the blade. It is not the revolution that destroys the machinery but the friction. ~ *Henry Ward Beecher*

The reason why worry kills more than work is that more people worry than work.

> ~ *Robert Frost*

——— WRINKLES ———

Wrinkles should merely indicate where smiles have been.   *~ Mark Twain*

——— WRITER ———

Every writer is a frustrated actor who recites his lines in the hidden auditorium of his skull.

~ Rod Sterling

The role of the writer is not to say what we can say, but what we are unable to say.

~ Anais Nin

Many people who want to be writers don't really want to be writers. They want to have been writers. They wish they had a book in print.

~ James Michener

I never desire to converse with a man who has written more books than he has read.

~ Samuel Johnson

If you would be a reader, read; if a writer, write.

~ Epictetus

In a very real sense, the writer writes in order to teach himself.   *~ Alfred Kazin*

Why do writers write? Because it isn't there.

~ *Thomas Berger*

Thinking is the activity I love best, and writing is simply thinking through my fingers.

~ *Isaac Asimov*

What no wife of a writer can ever understand is that a writer is working when he's staring out the window.

~ *Burton Rascoe*

—— **WRITING** ——

If you want to change the world, pick up your pen.

~ *Martin Luther*

To hold a pen is to be at war.

~ *Voltaire*

The pen is worse than the sword.

~ *Robert Burton*

The trouble with the publishing business is that too many people who have half a mind to write a book do so. ~ *William Targ*

Writing is the hardest way of earning a living, with the possible exception of wrestling alligators.

~ *Olin Miller*

Writing is the work of a slave.

~ *Charles H. Spurgeon*

Failure is very difficult for a writer to bear, but very few can manage the shock of early success.

~ *Maurice Valency*

Writing a book is an adventure. To begin with, it is a toy and an amusement. Then it becomes a mistress, then it becomes a master, then it becomes a tyrant. The last phase is that just as you are about to be reconciled to your servitude, you kill the monster, and fling him to the public. ~ *Winston Churchill*

I've always believed in writing without a collaborator, because where two people are writing the same book, each believes he gets all the worries and only half the royalties.　~ *Agatha Christie*

I never can understand how two men can write a book together; to me that's like three people getting together to have a baby.　~ *Evelyn Waugh*

Writing ... keeps me from believing everything I read.　~ *Gloria Steinem*

He who does not expect a million readers should not write a line.　~ *Goethe*

I write for myself and strangers. The strangers, dear Readers, are an afterthought.

~ *Gertrude Stein*

Your audience is one single reader. I have found that sometimes it helps to pick out one person—a real person you know, or an imagined person and write to that one.   *~ John Steinbeck*

The greatest part of a writer's time is spent in reading, in order to write; a man will turn over a half a library to make one book. *~ Samuel Johnson*

Unprovided with original learning, unformed in the habits of thinking, unskilled in the arts of composition, I resolve to write a book.

~ Edward Gibbon

There's nothing to writing. All you do is sit down at a typewriter and open a vein.

~ Red Smith

It helps to read the sentence aloud.

~ Harry Kemelman

If you want to get rich from writing, write the sort of thing that's read by persons who move their lips when they're reading to themselves.

~ Don Marquis

When you catch an adjective, kill it.

~ Mark Twain

I write the ending first. Nobody reads a book to get to the middle.   *~ Mickey Spillane*

Write freely and as rapidly as possible and throw the whole thing on paper. Never correct or rewrite until the whole thing is down. Rewrite in process is usually found to be an excuse for not going on.

~ John Steinbeck

I always begin with a character or characters, and then try to think up as much action for them as possible. *~ John Irving*

I always know the ending; that's where I start.

~ Toni Morrison

The last thing we decide in writing a book is what to put first. *~ Blaise Pascal*

Originality is nothing but judicious imitation. The most original writers borrowed from one another. The instruction we find in books is like fire. We fetch it from our neighbors, kindle it at home, communicate it to others, and it becomes the property of all.

~ Voltaire

About the most originality that any writer can hope to achieve honestly is to steal with good judgment.

~ Josh Billings

Action is character. *~ F. Scott Fitzgerald*

You can never know enough about your characters.

~ W. Somerset Maugham

A good title is the title of a successful book.

~ *Raymond Chandler*

I just think it's bad to talk about one's present work, for it spoils something at the root of the creative act. It discharges the tension. ~ *Norman Mailer*

Never talk about what you are going to do until after you have written it. ~ *Mario Puzo*

Don't tell anybody what your book is about and don't show it until it's finished. It's not that anybody will steal your idea but that all that energy that goes into the writing of your story will be dissipated.

~ *David Wallechinsky*

When I feel difficulty coming on, I switch to another book I'm writing. When I get back to the problem, my unconscious has solved it.

~ *Isaac Asimov*

A story should be a finished work before it is shown.

~ *Katherine Anne Porter*

First you're unknown, then you write one book and you move up to obscurity. ~ *Martin Myers*

Writing is easy. All you do is stare at a blank sheet of paper until drops of blood form on your forehead.

~ *Gene Fowler*

He writes so well he makes me feel like putting my quill back in my goose. ~ *Fred Allen*

Amuse the reader at the same time that you instruct him. ~ *Horace*

Someday I hope to write a book where the royalties will pay for the copies I give away.

~ *Clarence Darrow*

——— WRONG ———

One of the hardest things in this world to do is to admit you are wrong. And nothing is more helpful in resolving a situation than its frank admission.

The remedy for wrongs is to forget them.

~ *Publilius Syrus*

——— YAWN ———

A yawn is a silent shout. ~ *G.K. Chesterton*

——— YESTERDAY ———

Yesterday is a cancelled check; tomorrow is a promissory note; today is the only cash you have—so spend it wisely. ~ *Kay Lyons*

YOURSELF

Be yourself is about the worst advice you can give some people.

YOUTH

We are only young once. That is all society can stand.   *~ Bob Bowen*

Anyone who stops learning is old, whether at twenty or eighty. Anyone who keeps learning stays young. The greatest thing in life is to keep your mind young.

~ Henry Ford

Except for an occasional heart attack I feel as young as I ever did.   *~ Robert Benchley*

Youth is a wonderful thing. What a crime to waste it on children.   *~ George Bernard Shaw*

A youth with his first cigar makes himself sick; a youth with his first girl makes everybody sick.

~ Mary Little

I am not young enough to know everything.

~ James Barrie

Live as long as you can, the first twenty years are the longest half of your life.   *~ Southey*

——— ZOO ———

When I was a kid I said to my father one afternoon, "Daddy, will you take me to the zoo?" He answered, "If the zoo wants you let them come and get you."

~ *Jerry Lewis*

INDEX

344

348

Other Books by Bob Phillips

- World's Greatest Collection of Clean Jokes
- More Good Clean Jokes
- The Last of the Good Clean Jokes
- The Return of the Good Clean Jokes
- The All-American Joke Book
- The World's Greatest Collection of Heavenly Humor
- The World's Greatest Collection of Riddles and Daffy Definitions
- The World's Greatest Collection of Knock Knock Jokes and Tongue Twisters
- The Best of the Good Clean Jokes
- Wit and Wisdom
- Humor Is Tremendous
- The All New Clean Joke Book
- Good Clean Jokes for Kids
- Bible Fun
- Heavenly Fun
- In Search of Bible Trivia, Vol. 1
- In Search of Bible Trivia, Vol. 2
- The Little Book of Bible Trivia
- How Can I Be Sure? Premarital Inventory
- Anger Is a Choice
- Redi-Reference
- The Delicate Art of Dancing with Porcupines
- God's Hand Over Hume
- Praise Is a Three-Lettered Word—Joy
- The Handbook for Headache Relief

Dear Reader:

We would appreciate hearing from you regarding this Harvest House nonfiction book. It will enable us to continue to give you the best in Christian publishing.

1. What most influenced you to purchase *Positive Thinking for Positive Living?*
   - ☐ Author
   - ☐ Subject matter
   - ☐ Backcover copy
   - ☐ Recommendations
   - ☐ Cover/Title
   - ☐ _____

2. Where did you purchase this book?
   - ☐ Christian bookstore
   - ☐ General bookstore
   - ☐ Other
   - ☐ Grocery store
   - ☐ Department store

3. Your overall rating of this book:
   - ☐ Excellent
   - ☐ Fair
   - ☐ Very good
   - ☐ Poor
   - ☐ Good

4. How likely would you be to purchase other books by this author?
   - ☐ Very likely
   - ☐ Somewhat likely
   - ☐ Not very likely
   - ☐ Not at all

5. What types of books most interest you?
   (check all that apply)
   - ☐ Women's Books
   - ☐ Marriage Books
   - ☐ Current Issues
   - ☐ Self Help/Psychology
   - ☐ Bible Studies
   - ☐ Fiction
   - ☐ Biographies
   - ☐ Children's Books
   - ☐ Youth Books
   - ☐ Other _____

6. Please check the box next to your age group.
   - ☐ Under 18
   - ☐ 18-24
   - ☐ 25-34
   - ☐ 35-44
   - ☐ 45-54
   - ☐ 55 and over

Mail to: Editorial Director
Harvest House Publishers
1075 Arrowsmith
Eugene, OR 97402

Name _____

Address _____

City _____ State _____ Zip _____